Survive and Thrive
after Trauma

A personal account of life's journey when
alcoholism, divorce and death shatter the path

Susan Cowe

ISBN 978-0957548305

A catalogue record for this book is available from the British
Library

Cover design: with thanks to Jo Greenlees for technical help

Published by: Susan Cowe Books

'If your life is tumbling out of control and you want to better understand your feelings: reading this book is your first step. A great example where EFT and Matrix Reimprinting can help with extraordinary situations.'

Karl Dawson – Hay House author and Creator of Matrix Reimprinting

'A brave, courageous and must read book for anyone who feels trapped and unable to get out of a bad marriage or situation. Susan demonstrates quite clearly that until you clear those feelings and truly listen to yourself you are unlikely to move on. I highly recommend this easy to read book to anyone who wants to put their life back into perspective.'

Sheryl Andrews – Step by Step Listening. Accredited Clean Language Facilitator

'Susan has created an easy to read book to help you with emotional trauma. It is filled with nuggets of information and insights based on her experience and that of her contributors. If you are ready to change your life and be brave, let Susan's book help you on your new path.'

Karen Williams – Business Coach and author of *How to Stand Out in Your Business*

'A good read. A positive and honest account when living with considerable emotional distress. Not cruel or unkind. Full of helpful and informative advice too!'

Barbara Crick

'I highly recommend reading Susan's book. Having suffered my own disturbing traumas, I'm aware that without dealing with the actual memories, they will very likely come back at a later date to bite you. This book is full of really valuable information and resources. The story was quite something too. I was very eager to continue reading, and to take support from Susan's words.'

Tarryn Hunt – Founder of *Mums That Care*. Author of *365 Quotes for Mums that Care*

'Susan has made an excellent contribution to anyone who wishes to transform their own life after trauma. She candidly shares her own experience of trauma and presents tools and techniques to show others how they can move beyond their identity with their own story. This book is a great inspiration for anyone who wishes to end the trauma cycle.

Sasha Allenby - co-author of *Matrix Reimprinting Using EFT*.

Dedication

To the memory of my mother and father,

Madge and Bob Templeton.

Do you believe this of yourself?

I am what I am today
because of the choices I made yesterday.

Preface

This is a book of three parts: My life experience, an explanation section covering my chosen resources and a contributors section

Section 1: My story written in a relaxed style. When family life is steamrollered by alcoholism, divorce papers and death. I pepper it with humour, harsh advice and my take on the reality of life. Read, learn, share, implement and perhaps say 'it's time to let go.'

Section 2: The Resources and Explanations Section has an informative style. I briefly discuss the tools of my trade: Emotional Freedom Techniques (EFT), Matrix Reimprinting and Reiki: all of which I use as self-treating tools. I offer the opinion that EFT and Matrix therapy can benefit all emotional distress. I share explanations and lessons learned on a selection of emotive terminology and emotive situations. eg. anger, procrastination, forgiveness, alcoholism, grief: these topics are relevant for all areas of emotional anguish or distress.

Section 3: My Contributors section. I want my book to touch on a variety of trauma. These brave and generous people are thriving in a new unexpected place. Only Maria was a client. The others volunteered They share a little of their journey and the resources, support or mindset which specifically helped them. They send a positive message encouraging you to begin or to continue your journey to a better future.

Contents

Acknowledgements

Some of the people mentioned have helped me within my role as an EFT and Matrix Reimprinting Practitioner. Others have helped me write my book.

My appreciation goes to the following wonderful people:

Gary Craig, creator of EFT-1990s and Karl Dawson, creator of Matrix Reimprinting 2006 and Ted Wilmont, my EFT and Matrix Reimprinting trainer. Thanks Ted!

Sasha Allenby for her Matrix Reimprinting Webinar programme and my development training: 'Advanced Tools in Matrix Reimprinting'; Ortal Pelleg for helping me on my *guinea pig* session at 'Advanced Tools in Matrix Reimprinting'; Philip Davis and Christine Sutton PTT (Picture Tapping Technique); Jane Russell who introduced me to EFT and Natasha Abduahrum Black. I use her version of the Emotional Scale.

Four friends who read part of the book and gave the thumbs up: Tarryn Hunt of Mums That Care, Barbara Crick of Emsworth Cookery School, Anne Klepacz a neighbour, and Sheryl Andrews of Step by Step Listening, an accredited Clean Language Facilitator with whom I learnt Clean Language skills.

Paula Bishop, my Matrix swap partner who teaches me Donna Eden's Energy Exercises; Raymond Aaron whose 10-10-10 Program I followed to write the book; Jo Greenlees, graphic designer and Illustrator who helped with my book cover and Christina Harkness, my copy editor, who deserves a gracious "thank you".

Lucy Whittington of Being a Business Celebrity who got me

doing my thing and Natalie March, my physiotherapist.

Herb Miller for *being there,* helping with technology and soothing me when necessary. Thank you for your support and your love. I love you.

My two 'big' children. I hope you will be proud of me. I love you both, equally. I hope you will understand that there is a *bigger picture* in all of this.

My other family members who, well … I don't know what you think! I love you all.

My Contributors. Thank you for sharing your positive message.

My thanks of course to my clients – I wish you continued success and freedom!

Section 1
Our story
Introduction

This book begins with the story of two people who started married life together in the time when it wasn't chucked away after a couple of arguments though I doubt the players assumed it would end the way it did.

The main purpose of the book is

- to give hope, inspiration and energy to those who have been wounded by life and may doubt their future.

- to believe and understand that life can change out of all recognition, and for the better.

- to hope a joy is just ahead of you: baby steps can get you there.

- to give realisation that you can permit, allow and believe that you can heal.

It is not meant to cover all bases. I do not suggest one size fits all. This book will be scattered with 'signs', scattered with humour, and warmth too.

So why am I writing this book? I always knew I had this book 'inside' me. The one I assumed would always stay there, tucked inside.

I could **choose** to stay safe. Not allow this book to be available to the discerning, critical and vast public. Hold it inside.

The last statement is quite important and relevant.

If it stays 'inside', what is the benefit of that? Negative memories and emotions are potentially damaging to mental and physical health.

Vitally, I do believe I have something of value to share.

The title is 'Survive and Thrive after Trauma'. What is 'Trauma'? It is:

- a wound or injury
- emotional shock producing a lasting effect upon a person.

I am writing about the latter. I chose the simplest definition I could find. I intend this book to be simple to read and to understand.

To survive and thrive after an emotional trauma requires some form of action to be taken to remedy a situation. You have to choose to take action. You will see the word and the suggestion to choose on several occasions.

'Choose and Choice'. These words are fundamental to how I work with my Emotional Freedom Techniques® (EFT) based therapy. I believe many people do not appreciate or realise that there is always a choice in how we live or continue to live our life.

Therefore, we all have choice. No one can take that away from us. It is in our hands.

I also believe it is wrong to expect others to always be there to help us with our 'mess'. Sadly, it doesn't matter whether the mess was in no way, shape or form our fault. We only gain strength when we have managed to recover from it ourselves.

In 2001 my comfortable, although not always harmonious

life, started to feel decidedly unpleasant and unattractive. By early 2003, it was stunningly altered beyond all recognition.

The journey and decision to write my book was actually quite sudden. The complete laziness which I had always assumed was the reason for not sharing (or 'airing' dirty linen!) was turned on its head. The time was right. Quite suddenly, or be it the *Law of Attraction*, I attended Stephanie Hale's Millionaire Boot camp for Authors.

Three days into the event I reported home that I had failed to save any money that day as I had invested in a programme to help me write my first book. To me it was a complete 'no brainer'.

- I had this book inside me.
- It was really starting to hold me back.
- I knew I could do it.
- I wanted it done and out of the way.

So who am I to think I can offer hope, encouragement, belief to others? Who am I indeed!

I choose to quote from 'Our Deepest Fear' by Marianne Williamson:

*"Our deepest fear is not that we are inadequate. Our deepest fear is that we are powerful beyond measure. It is our light, not our darkness that most frightens us. We ask ourselves, 'Who am I to be brilliant, gorgeous, talented, fabulous?' Actually, who are you **not** to be?"*

So who am I?

I am an Emotional Well-being Practitioner and work in the field of psychotherapy.

I work primarily with Emotional Freedom Techniques (EFT) and Matrix Reimprinting, 'psychological acupuncture', 'the tapping therapy'. I use these techniques to relieve stress and anxiety and to clear deeply hidden negative beliefs. My aim is to increase confidence levels.

I may suddenly become humorous at inappropriate times. Humour is necessary – laughs to move us out of the deeper dread or fear.

There is a great scene in the film 'Steel Magnolias' the funeral scene[1]. I laughed, cried, was surprised; many emotional reactions within that sequence.

Humour, a reality check – call it what you want, can be vital if we are affected by trauma or upset. Otherwise, we become self- obsessed, over indulgent and feel sorry for ourselves for far too much of the time. That said, it is hard to forget the bad events one has experienced. However, it is not a prerequisite to life's path that we are bound by them. With the kind of life experience I will be sharing with you, it is quite hard to forget or block events when you have children. You have a constant reminder.

My daughter questioned that statement. My belief is that in the early years after 2003, perhaps I could have booted those memories 'into touch' if I hadn't had the children. I could have tried to block the 'nasty stuff". But we were all

---

[1] See "I Wanna know Why"
www.starpulse.com/Movies/Steel_Magnolias/Great_Film_Mome
nts/

in this together. In time we would choose to address our pain in our own individual way and I prefer to remember the good times: the healthier choice.

You will see words written in **bold**. These words have their own place of importance in the Resources Section. I try to give acceptable meaning to the emotive words and to portray how those feelings may keep us in a place of negativity. To move forward positively we need to release the hold that certain emotions have on us.

So why might this book be of benefit and value to you?

- A big trauma to one person is a small trauma to another.
- A small trauma to one person is a big trauma to another.

Trauma is very personal and individual.

For those of you who have 'come out the other side' and are reading this, I wish to share and celebrate with you as we continue positively on our life's journey.

I will have certain words and phrases repeated throughout the book. Repetition of a fact can help change mindset.

When I started writing this book, I wrote a note to myself: Am I airing 'dirty linen' and if so why? Could I not just keep all this to myself?

During a tea break, I turned the radio on and received a sign. The Four Tops were singing 'Reach Out, I'll Be

There'[2]

Some interesting words in there. Have a look – the song about the gremlins – the self-doubt.

I also gave myself some stick-beating angst around the possibility that I can or may hurt a small number of people. Three of them are the most important people in my life. I feel an area of **responsibility**. In this case, I most definitely should be aware of a responsibility. This has not stopped me. I will not be using the important people's names. By not using their names, it does suggest a lack of warmth, but privacy is vital.

Fundamental to the book is the understanding that we are only responsible to ourselves. Illness, death, divorce, whatever ghastly situation that befalls us, we adults are only responsible *to* and *for* ourselves. We cannot be responsible for the actions of others. And ... we should not expect others to be responsible for us.

So I am not permitting **self-sabotage** to stop me. By that, I mean the feelings that make you or me nervous or anxious.

- The 'Should I do this? Oh, best not do it.'
- 'A silly idea: who am I to think I can accomplish this?'
- Or worse still: 'They'll all laugh at me.'

Interestingly, after I had finished the first draft of the book, I suffered a trapped nerve in my right elbow. Now this could have been a sign to:

---

[2] www.elyrics.net/read/f/four-tops-lyrics/reach-out-i_ll-be-there-lyrics.html

1. Stop and forget the whole thing.
2. Take a rest from writing and allow quiet and clarity to be given a place – to do a proper job.

I chose Number 2. I trust that my loved ones will understand.

Signs: we can take what we like when we receive *signs*, so you'll get my take on it. I have always thought that I am quite unobservant but highly intuitive. We'll see. Cynics can say what they will about signs or messages. However, they are out there for us to act on.

With regard to my Contribution Section key lessons learned are passed on to you. These people have moved on and are thriving.

Emotional pain is still seen as a weakness: 'Put on a brave face.' 'It will be better soon.'

I prefer to say that a quiet cry or a roaring of rage can be truly beneficial. Too many suffer in silence … or is this really just a British thing? I welcome your comments.

Now to Chapter 1, The Golden Years.

Chapter 1
The Golden Years –
not through rose coloured spectacles!

We met in the seventies and had great fun studying and living the student life in Edinburgh. What memories! The first time we met he was 'worse for wear', but so were many of us! Life was for having fun.

That night when walking home, he asked if I would go to his twenty-first birthday party. I asked when it was.

'In May' came the answer, in a matter of fact tone. That was six months away. We laughed. That was a challenge! Would we still be seeing each other then?

As he left me at my hall of residence, I asked his full name. He told me and I asked his friends who were with us if he was bullshitting. 'No, it's not bullshit. It is Cowe; pronounced C O W, not Crowe, or Cowie.'

We married in 1976 and enjoyed setting up home, starting our jobs and embracing all that life was offering.

Two years later we moved to the Scottish Borders, got Sam our Border Collie and really enjoyed our time there.

Our next move was very brave but hugely exciting. We moved to the Middle Eastern state of Qatar the 1980s. He worked on a school and I worked in a school. He was Consultant Engineer for a school building programme. I taught in the Doha Independent School.

I loved most of my time there. A down time was when I

suffered an ectopic pregnancy. We loved the weather, the lifestyle and the money. I remember it took me some time to settle back here in England on our return. We came back because he correctly believed his career would suffer if we stayed longer than the four years. He was a structural engineer considering his career. It was the right decision.

At this point, our son was a baby. He was born in the UK and spent his first year in Qatar. Our daughter arrived the year after our return home.

We were both busy and just getting on with life. Nothing out of the ordinary.

This chapter title: 'The Golden Years' urges me to comment that they were happy times and not seen through rose coloured spectacles. Our children's strength and character show that it was normal family life. They are lovely young people.

We lived in the historic town of Marlow on the River Thames and made a few very good friends. I actually made good friends with three particular women. Twenty years later they were there for me at the end, when my husband made his exit from this world.

Chapter 2
Needing pats on the back, or did I really need them?

Life journeyed on. From a professional point of view, I started my supply teaching when our daughter was one year old and our son three. When I think about that, I laugh. Carting a double buggy, travel cot and the bag to the child minders. My God, what a carry on! My husband travelled at rush hour to his job and I organised family life. It was what needed to be done.

He progressed in his career but always had a grumble at how he didn't really care for his boss. He didn't really care for any of his bosses. I'm afraid that was a bit tiresome for me to hear a lot of the time.

At some point, we all got bicycles and we would go for little cycle rides. However, the pattern soon fell that the kids and I would cycle to meet Dad at the pub. He cycled there earlier. The kids and I would have a pub sandwich and then the three of us would cycle back, leaving him for longer. This was our weekend 'stuff'. I can't say I'm particularly proud of that now but I can consider that the cycling was good exercise; the pub was in a lovely location; I chatted to friends; I and didn't have to make lunch.

The children grew and life was fine.

I did get 'cheesed off' with him stating every now and then that he did not feel appreciated. I remember thinking, 'Well, I'm a working mum and I'm not really appreciated either!'

He occasionally would get upset and say we did not respect him. Hell, I was doing my bit too. Funny how that part can often be forgotten in a relationship.

I wonder how many of you have also thought that? I am of course looking at it from a woman's point of view. Do men still try to demand respect? Assume it is their right? Beat themselves on the chest like a gorilla? Think, 'I need to feel respected as the bread winner?'

These age-old beliefs are deeply entrenched in the psyche. No wonder it's a squabbling point nowadays because the situation has almost reversed.

Men are probably very wary about questioning their position in a relationship because women are now so very strident.

A few decades ago did most women assume, myself included that we just get on with our stuff, and if clever and smart enough, be able to keep our mouths shut and not challenge? Give our husband the pat on the back, a blow job or whatever else provided the solution to soothe his ego?

Anyway, it used to piss me off.

Chapter 3
An affair and I didn't listen properly

This stage of events unfolded around my fortieth birthday. I remember because I told my mother later that year that although he had tried hard with arranging a surprise for me, the event itself was marred in many ways.

The chapter title says it all: An affair and I didn't listen properly.

We were not listening to each other. I now believe many couples may have very little idea how to communicate or listen properly to each other. However, at the hotel where we celebrated my fortieth birthday, I remember being humiliated and embarrassed by him at the dinner table. He ridiculed me in front of the waiter. In my memory of the incident it appeared like a TV sketch of an arrogant dominating man making a fool of a pathetic mousy wife when she couldn't decide what to choose on the menu. Hindsight is an amazing thing and I suppose he may have been feeling strained about a build-up to *something* and perhaps concerned about it. Who knows? I don't. That was maybe the first time I was aware that drink could make him behave badly, in a really unpleasant way.

If that happened today the drink will be poured over the head and an impressive stomping out of the restaurant would be par for the course.

Afterwards, when I thought of my fortieth birthday, the feeling was not a pleasant one.

The next few months were tricky. Time fogs the memories.

The balance of our stable relationship had shifted.

Around Christmas time rather than go to the pub I chose to watch a film I'd been eager to see. 'Last of the Mohicans' with Daniel Day Louis. Daniel was just great in that film. It still keeps me happy every time I watch it.

When he returned I remember he casually dropped something into the conversation about a particular woman who went there too.

'That woman is actually making me feel a bit uncomfortable. Can't you come to the pub more often so that she sees we are a close family?'

I was only half listening and still visualising Daniel wearing almost nothing and running about the beautifully scenic countryside.

My reaction to his statement was along the lines: 'Oh, for goodness sake, just deal with it. She knows we're a family unit. She sees us there. Deal with it! Why do you need me to sort it out? I don't want to have to keep going to the pub for that reason.'

She was in my mind, an older woman and frankly, although she held a good opinion of herself, I just dismissed it.

When my son was a teenager, an older teenager, I used to warn him about older women, but not for the reasons you may think!

However niggling suspicions did pop into my head over the next few weeks. At the same time I had been offered a supply teaching contract which meant I had to accept one term of full-time work: The summer term. This school often gave me a short period of part-time work. We debated whether this was really a good idea.

We discussed with the children what would be involved.

I was aware that I would be unable to do all I used to do at home. I had always avoided any full-time teaching. I have felt pressure when expected to do something fairly challenging. I needed to think about it first. When I accepted the post I was fine with the idea. Yes, we could all benefit.

The children were asked to take on special jobs for which they would be paid. My husband did his job as normal. I just worked a full teaching week.

It worked. I was focused. The jobs were done. But I must have forgotten to pat him on the back. I must have missed praising him. I must have assumed we were a team, pulling together. I must have assumed he was also just waiting until the end of the school term and for our summer holiday. I must assume that I neglected him by being focused and earning more money for us all that summer.

One of the things I need to 'tap' on should the trigger be pressed, is being made a fool of.

I sit here feeling quite angry.

People who know me know I swear occasionally. I have always found it to be a great release of pressure. Those more gentle souls may criticise but when someone makes a fool of you, we all react in different ways.

I was fucking angry when I realised what was going on.

I had my suspicions that summer term. I had been watching 'things' in the pub during the spring. Was I imagining that he was behaving differently?

Just before the end of term, I tackled the situation. I asked him if he was having an affair and was of course told that I was 'off my head' to think such a stupid thing. I raised the subject frequently and was angrily told to stop being so stupid.

Readers, if you think your partner is having an affair, and with all the discussions around it, be very suspicious if you are told you are off your head, that you are behaving in a ridiculous way.

I found myself sitting in the corner of the kitchen floor crying and wondering how on earth I got myself into this state. I must be cracking up.

I also suggest if your partner buys him or herself new underwear unexpectedly then I ask you to enter the real world, take your head out your arse and have a good old think!

I had been working much harder and agonised if I had been hopelessly misreading the situation. But the fucker had bought new underwear!

When a marriage is in trouble, stress and anxiety can keep you in a hyper state.

Here are some observations relating to this part in the story:

- When I was in this state of mistrusting myself and my intuition, I was trusting him to do the *right thing.*

- Why on earth would he throw our family life aside? I better pull myself together.

- I was thinking I have a job to do – I can't go on thinking like this, I'll make myself ill.

- Why can we not hear or see?

A possible answer is because it's too painful, so we ignore it.

I did follow him in the car on a couple of occasions. I think I felt disgusted with myself at the time for doing this. But I knew I was right. I was also trying to find out what the 'odd' telephone number was on his mobile. This was *early days* – mobiles and technology have never really been my thing but a friend of mine helped me.

She found out who the person was and I had been right. It was 'the older woman'. He had tried to tell me months ago.

- Did he try to tell me because he wanted to re-ignite our relationship?
- Was he warning me to smarten up my ideas because another person was interested in him?
- Should I blame myself for not listening?

Screw that notion! Yes I could accept it as my fault but my self-esteem was not that low!

He had chosen to introduce the kids and me to her one day when we were leaving to cycle home after a Saturday lunch at the pub. Christ knows what she thought. He, I realised later, would then go off with her for a couple of hours.

Anyway, this is a bit of 'dirty linen' but relevant. To me it is because for those struggling with marital or partnership issues, the mental anguish when a relationship goes wrong, is very strong. It is also very bad for **physical health.** Later I realised I had a natural, intuitive understanding of what may be helpful and necessary for me. Destructive and damaging emotions are very bad for physical health. Hence a need for Reiki a few years later.

The day that I found out who she was, with my friend's help, was the eve of our summer holiday to France.

My friend had done the 'stupid phone call bit' for me. You know, the 'Oh I must have the wrong number. Actually, could you help me with ...'

There was no point me telephoning and trying to find out who she was. When I telephone someone, my voice seems to be highly recognisable. I still laugh and say that there would be no point in me anonymously phoning an agony aunt or uncle on a radio programme because someone would hear and say, 'Oh, there's Susan again trying to sort out her problems.'

I told my friend that I was going round to see this other woman. She offered to come with me but I was very comfortable to go alone. The kids were at a play camp. I did ask her for a whisky though.

Even I have times when a drink can kill the stress levels whether it's 10 a.m. in the morning or not. I downed a whisky and set off. The rest of the day went like this:

I was feeling **anger**, rage, fury. I had been made a fool of. Yes anger and pain and hurt. Bugger fear. Female instinct to protect her young and herself took over. But I kept my cool – I was in control.

I have always found it strange that I can worry at times over stupid little things, but when a big issue rises in front of me – I can deal with it. I went round to her posh house, could not find the front door, so went round to the back of the house, walked through her garden and knocked on the door. It was of no importance to me if her husband was in or not. I could not have cared less. As it happens, he wasn't in.

I got straight to the point. I asked her if she was having an affair with my husband. Of course she denied it. I left after a few minutes. However, she had given something away in the conversation.

'Oh, Susan, we are only pub friends. If I was ever in Reading we would meet for lunch occasionally. ' That was news to me!

I had behaved impeccably even though I was wanted to smash her face in but I kept composed and held onto my dignity one hundred per cent.

I did the holiday packing and in the early evening the children and I went to the pub to meet Daddy. The children who were ten and eight, knew that Mummy wasn't happy but I don't think that they had any inkling of what Mummy and Daddy had been squabbling about over the last few weeks.

The pub was fine – for everyone else. My husband had no idea what I'd done that day. She came in. It was as if nothing out of the ordinary was happening.

I observed. You would never have known that two women in that room were feeling uneasy, angry or even confident.

We left earlier than usual. After all, we were going on holiday. The kids went to bed, the car was packed and then I told him. I told him what I had done that morning and what she had said. He could not believe I had gone to her house. Was I not afraid her husband would be there? Was I fuck! Couldn't have given a shit!

We had been married twenty years. He did not have a clue what I was capable of nor intelligent enough to work it out.

Straight away, he said, 'All right, what do you want to happen? It's over with her from this moment. What do you want to happen? I haven't slept with her.'

I told him if I had been her, I would have slept with him.

What a prat he was. I remember he looked at me with a strange expression when I said that. As if it surprised him, I suppose.

But I knew that I wanted 'us' back.

We went on holiday. It gave us a fresh start. It was certainly not without its pain while things got sorted out but it most definitely gave us a fresh start in all respects. It was good for us. And we became very close and happy to find each other again.

Chapter 4
Self-employment! Brave but ... be careful if you work from home

Within a few months of all of that, he decided being self-employed could be the way ahead. He was very frustrated, always critical of having a boss. Not only that, he certainly believed he could run his own business.

Some years later, people said they were fairly gobsmacked that he had done it. After all, his children were not yet teenagers and the responsibility and the stress would have scared many others off. But ... it was the right move.

It was a move that he was able to handle professionally. He chose to work from home: we could not afford office space. We had a room which we could change into the office; the children's play room. It was exciting, and his first client phoned him within his first week. His client base had moved with him. However, isolation, and my belief and understanding that home was no longer a place of peace for him, took its toll.

I am working from home myself now. Do I feel lonely or isolated? No, I have a busy life that's too full most of the time. I cram loads into it and my grumble is that I could do with some more peace and calm time. I had better take note of that!

I am trying not to make this all *me*, but I was part of this. My job was to do the bits of paperwork, invoicing, letters to clients etc. There was an assumption that we worked as a team. However, in time, I realised that this 'rabbit hutch' space wasn't too good for me. I was still doing my supply teaching three days a week, so I sacked myself and suggested that he get a *girl* to help him. This should have happened. This would have eased things, but he only used people to help occasionally, not on a regular basis. This caused some pressure.

From a success point of view the money came in straight away. Not the big bucks, but he was successful. He was good at what he did. People respected and trusted in his ability. It is a brave move to work from home. This was about 1997. Nowadays, there is better understanding of the isolation felt by some home workers. He had a good routine. He would get up and be in his office by 8.30.

He relaxed by going to the pub at lunchtimes (he skipped breakfast) for an hour or so. He ate lunch when he returned. Our daughter was keen on Food Technology at school and would chastise him about his eating habits. He would go to the pub in the early evening for an hour or so. This was the respite, and the downfall.

Psychologically, working from home can be isolating. It is an issue for many people. So how did I deal with this new routine? How supportive was I? As I mentioned I sacked myself early on. I knew that the marriage was doomed if we were in that little room for long and I knew I needed my own space. Unfortunately, he didn't want to pay someone else to do that job. The family team work was the idea however I didn't want to be dictated to and saw the potential dangers. I wanted my space. I needed to be my own person. I assumed that we should respect each other's wishes. I appreciated he had his stresses over self-employment but I was not at his beck and call.

Assuming anything is dangerous. Talking to each other is a more sensible idea. Confrontational perhaps but better to have it discussed. I was always going to help but I could not be the *Girl Friday* that he was looking for. I expect he felt let down by that.

The film 'Sliding Doors' looks at the possibility that your life can take two routes. Which route? How is it decided?

If I had chosen the 'Don't be your own person route – the family needs us working as a team' route, where would I be now? How would that have worked out?

One day I was having a coffee and a moan with a good friend who was in a similar position to me with regards to a partner heavily reliant on alcohol. Her child was younger than ours. She said, 'You know, I think he's a control freak!'

I paused – I was surprised! I had never thought about it like that. We had a life together; you adapt to each other but when I thought about it, 'Yeah! He couldn't handle me going up to Edinburgh every now and then.' I had a wonderful excuse to go up to Edinburgh two or three times a year. My mother was up there and in not the best of health. My God was that an issue?

I have also considered how some women possibly behave when they've been in a marriage which has lasted a considerable time. We were together nine years before the children. We both desperately wanted our children and once the children arrived it was wonderful.

Suddenly some years had passed and the children were

growing up. They were more self-sufficient and Mummy was able to consider:

I've got some more free time. I can do other things.

It's like having a different role. A different aspect of life could be seen. I was very much aware that I wanted 'me time', and 'our time' wasn't fulfilling me. When I say 'our time' I mean just going to the pub.

I could have been more imaginative with my activities with the children. Especially perhaps with my daughter. My son had his rugby. I don't know what I thought, but I would still go to the pub quite often. The affair was over and I was never going to allow someone else to stop me frequenting the pub. I never once considered I had a drink problem myself. I would just go for a couple every now and then, probably twice a week. However, I was aware that I was becoming frustrated by my lack of gumption, and at the same time all of a sudden, I found out that he was drinking more. I may be talking two or three years into self-employment before I became aware. And, it was a surprise!

He thought he was capable of being self-employed; without question he was very capable. He was very good at what he did but the stress and the strain of self-employment and the administration issues ate into him. With hindsight there were procedures which could have been put in place

- a person to help with the administration
- a move to an office.

And the drink just took a quiet hold. Insidious and strong.

Chapter 5
The writing on the wall – big black and strong, but not when you don't want to see it

Things were not rosy and even a couple of years before our twenty-fifth wedding anniversary, during a consultation with my doctor I had flippantly remarked that I hoped I could hang in till my silver anniversary as I felt I deserved a bloody good holiday!

She said, 'Not you two as well!'

She liked him and they had a good chat the odd time he went into the surgery. She said structural engineering was so different to doctoring and she would chat away with him.

She told me later that she could not get through to him health wise. And that most of the time he just talked about how the children and I were all that mattered. Well I suppose I have to believe that. I doubt he would lie to her.

I must say that I really enjoyed my twenty-fifth wedding anniversary holiday. It was a trip to Rome. I was stunned by Rome. I loved it!

But the year of that anniversary in 2001 was the time I started to find spirit bottles hidden in his rolled-up structural drawings.

I wonder now why he hid the bottles. It was not only me who found them. My daughter would challenge him too about his drinking but that did not stop him either. Why would someone hide a bottle in a rolled-up plan and not throw it deep into the dustbin? Perhaps it was a cry for help.

Every two to three months I would challenge him about the drink escalation. A good old row ensued. I suppose I thought I might get through to him. When your two children are stuck in the middle, the psychology behind your husband's excessive drinking doesn't matter. You just want him to stop as it is hurting everyone. When the rows got worse, he would say to the children, 'Your mother will never leave me. She's better off here.'

I could feel a little self-disgust about that statement because most certainly there was truth in it. I had no intention of leaving; I was not the one doing anything wrong. So I agonised over 'the will I won't I leave' for a long time.

Finances would have been tight. The house would have to be sold. He worked from home and I might have to leave with the children. He was not going to move out.

The easy answer was to ignore it as much as possible, pretend it wasn't really that damaging. I would ignore it for long spells at a time.

Isn't it a bloody good job that we don't know what is round the corner?

There is a big issue over **Secondary Gain** in a situation like this.

As I write this in my beautiful 'long' room, the room where I work with my clients, overlooking the garden, with the sun shining, early on a summer morning, I can only shrug my shoulders. ... C'est la vie! Wow ...

What else is it? It's life and it's a journey. We have to live for today.

Around six years after he died, when I was having Counselling sessions due to perhaps a bout of mild depression, it is hardly surprising that I discovered I probably had a **'responsibility'** issue.

I feel sure that I felt it was my responsibility to help him and sort it out.

I have worked over time to accept that I am only responsible for me. My children are now big children – adults if you prefer. I like to class them affectionately as my 'big children'.

I am not responsible for anyone else. I cannot try to protect or change someone else. It is not my right. It is not my duty.

Life went on. He worked and drank. I collected the empty bottles and threw them out occasionally. I had my job-share at school for which I am eternally grateful. The children lived in an increasingly unhappy home. I also mentioned to my mother that I really did have a big problem on my hands because his drinking was escalating.

Not the best of times.

Chapter 6
Out of my shell … and it was good

2001 was a build-up to 2002 and it all rolled into one. At the time of writing this book, I was also wondering if the next couple of chapters needed to be so graphic. I decided it should all stay. This is my story and it has to be told in the best way possible.

In the spring of that year, I finally succeeded in getting my husband to detox. Certainly not one of my easier jobs. He needed help to change habits. He needed guidance. He agreed that he needed help. He was unhappy with his situation and realised this was what was necessary.

He was concerned though that people would then know he had a drink problem.

Oh, the tragedy of: 'What will people think?'

There is nothing much to say about that statement. It damages many potentially rescuable situations. Kills the 'get out of jail free' chance. It is also a great excuse for many to just keep on going along a path to destruction. **Procrastination!**

The date the detox started was the time our son was doing major school exams. I was pissed off with that. I thought it selfish. At stressful times, it is difficult to know what is right or wrong. You stagger on from one thing to another in your own personal state and deal with it.

He still went to the pub at lunchtimes but drank orange juice instead of beer.

I expect he was trying to keep his routine, his chats, his

socialising. Sadly though, 'alcohol dependency' is a big thing to deal with. Lifestyle changes are fundamental. Transformation is necessary.

It was messy and a shitty time. He was trying to succeed and in my mind, I was trying to keep a quiet calm home so that he could be as stress free as possible. I often think it unbelievable that I 'didn't lose it' and go crazy. Later, he said he thought I was not supportive enough. I must have been expected to be like a fucking nanny. He told me that I did not know how to behave.

As I write this, I find that statement unbelievable: 'I did not know how to behave.'

Imagine my saying that:

- I do not know how to behave to keep him happy.
- I do not know how to behave to keep him on the path to recovery.
- I do not know how to behave to get us out of this mess.

Who did I think I was? Some kind of saint?

(Oops the stick and anger monkey surfaced.)

No, just someone who imagined that 'things might get better for us all'.

One day, when it was near the end of his first attempted detox, my son asked, 'Mum, what can you do to make sure Dad doesn't start drinking again?'

I did not have an answer and only shook my head.

He detoxed with the help of the Addiction Counselling

Trust (ACT) in High Wycombe. During the detox programme I was surprised when I was given the opportunity to attend counselling sessions, or chats, as an 'abused' wife; part of my husband's treatment.

The other women sitting around the table were mothers of drug users. I was the only one there with an alcohol related problem. Gosh, I felt sorry for them. Emotional blackmail. Their sons had promised to quit. They had hurt them emotionally and in some cases physically and they had stolen from them.

You are given this chance to talk with others who are in a similar situation. He had his own counsellor. I had mine. It really opened my eyes. The counsellor suggested I wrote a list of reasons to stay in the abusive situation and another of reasons to leave the abusive situation.

A surprise: I had a choice. I could weigh up the pros and cons. When I was living in a messy situation, I certainly did not really consider the fact that I had a choice. I had my work. 'Praise be the Lord!' I had my work. I had our children. I had a situation that needed to be dealt with but I hadn't really considered 'a get out clause'.

I did write my two lists. The list to leave was so much longer than the list to stay.

My husband was blindingly furious when he heard I could get some help from his ACT Support team. He did not trust it would all be confidential from one counsellor to the other. Either that or the 'control freak trigger' was asserting itself.

On one occasion, eight months later when he was on the second detox, I was offered the opportunity to sit in on the session with the counsellor. The sessions took place at our home. I was surprised to be given this opportunity but I was fine with it. What a crock of shit he was telling her. To me he was dreaming. He looked quite pathetic speaking about our dreams for the future. He sat and spoke about how we were working together on this. How he had dreams to do this, that and the other.

At this second detox stage I had dictated my terms to delaying the divorce proceedings. They were clear to me. He was to move his office out of the house. He was to start making plans for this to happen. If he achieved this and kept off the booze I may then accept that a delay to potential divorce could be considered. I was very angry and let it be known to the counsellor. I remember thinking that the counsellor could so easily have been in some personal danger, being in a volatile situation like that.

In June 2002 about six weeks into the first detox programme, I went to Paris with a very good friend. We had booked this some months before. I knew I deserved a holiday, away from him. I needed something to look forward to. He was actually in quite good form when I left.

During my three days in Paris, I had growing anxieties about the nature of the texts between us.

On my return, he had the dinner ready but was 'worse for wear'. I could not really believe it.

My (our) friend was saddened too. It was ghastly. I can only assume he did it to punish me. I should not have left him to his own devices.

Now who is feeling paranoid?

My son later said he thought it was a bit of father and son

bonding maybe. My son was sixteen. He had suggested taking my son to the pub. To relapse that way was one hell of a slap in the face.

He had started and continued to drink again. Not surprisingly, it has taken some time to deal with my **anger**. I was confused, let down and really cheesed off.

It was now summer. I am not going to offer up too much detail about this next part but I had a lovely time, briefly. Someone I knew. Someone I knew would not trouble me with regard to a long term relationship.

A glorious and exciting 'fling'. The stuff they write about in books. Wonderful! It was fun, dangerous and just what I needed. It very probably saved my sanity, or my going to the doctor for pills. It made me feel attractive, young and good!

My husband knew nothing about it. He was totally unaware. He was already in a much worse place than before. Potentially, he could have easily found out but I suppose it just never entered his head. He would have actually been astounded. Just as well. That's all folks, on that part.

In early autumn, things were not good. I went away with a friend to her mobile home on two weekends. I had to stay with a friend on another couple of occasions. I had to get away. At that time when the rows got too much, I just wanted to escape to a hotel.

One time when I tried to get away, he sat on the car bonnet outside the house, in front of all the neighbours.

What a carry on. Unbelievable that physical violence did not take over and be part of the collapse. He was drunk and I did shut the car window on him as he tried to get the car keys whereupon he shouted, 'Assault!'

If I am to be cynical, I expect that he wanted me to assault him so that he could 'use' it later.

Stressful and awful.

I did have the understanding that I was dealing with someone who was very dependent on **alcohol**. I was aware I needed to keep my cool.

I would go to Francesco's coffee shop – a place of peace. I would sit with all my paperwork, not J.K. Rowling style, but trying to get some clarity of thought, outside the home. I tried to figure out the expenses, the possibilities – everything to do with me and the children being able to stay in the house and … getting him out.

A black time …

Then it was oh, so easy.

Chapter 7
Him or me in the 'nuthouse'.
I chose for it not to be me

In late autumn, I finally got my husband to agree to marriage guidance counselling. I really liked her. He didn't. She came recommended by someone. It's a good idea to go to someone who is recommended.

We went twice together then he refused to go back. I went alone for the third visit. When the session was over and I was just leaving I believe she was confiding in me, trying to help me understand my situation better because she said, 'You know, I don't think separation is a secure enough option. I think you should consider a more formal decision to safeguard yourself and the children.'

I just looked at her blankly then the penny dropped. It had to be divorce. I drove home weeping thinking, quite clearly, 'Look what you're making me do, you fool.'

I felt sick.

A subtle change had taken place. I then closed down emotionally. There was no more time to delay the inevitable. It became as clear as day.

If I didn't take action, one of us would end up in the nuthouse.[3]

I chose for it not to be me.

_____

[3] This statement is key to where I am today. On more than one occasion it has been suggested I choose another word rather than nuthouse. However that is exactly how I felt.

I could end this part of the book now. I could stop 'airing dirty linen' but it's not possible because what happened shortly after is vital.

During this writing process, someone close to me hinted that perhaps the idea of 'brushing it under the carpet' was a consideration.

Yes, of course, it was, but then I would be like countless others. For some reason I seem to feel I have something to offer to those struggling emotionally. To those who have this kind of scenario playing in the background of their life.

I did not go through this writing without feelings of angst but I really tried to work through them. I felt 'emotionally bullied' on occasions whilst writing this and that is the whole point.

Sadly, I had put up with emotional bullying before. I can only trust that my refusal to be emotionally bullied, and my desire to write this part of my life in this book, will not have unfortunate results for me. What I mean is that I hope those close to me will understand that this book may, just may, give others the energy to take their next step when they're thinking, 'How much crap am I supposed to take?'

I return to the statement I made earlier about feeling physically sick when I realised that I had only one option: a subtle change had occurred.

I had closed down emotionally to consider clearly what to do. Closed and protected by my invisible shell. What a lovely safe place that is. I could write a book about the pros and cons of that simple statement. This was definitely the time for me to be 'cocooned in my shell' and not allow anyone in.

In hindsight, (wow, isn't hindsight a great thing! So many things we learn from hindsight. Gosh, wouldn't our lives be dull if we had hindsight to protect us?) little did I know that the death of my marriage was actually the first death I dealt with.

The death of my marriage – the realisation that it was:

Either him or me – him or me going to the nuthouse.

- I chose for it not to be me.
- I chose to survive.
- I stopped caring about him

I was not going to allow him to destroy me. I had spent the previous months:

- being responsible
- trying to keep us together
- doing what was best for kids

So fuck it. Fuck it all! I chose me. We will be fine and I am leaving the 'sinking ship'.

I have worked hard on **anger** as a result of this 'jolly romp' which is part of my life. Anger is usually a mask for fear, pain or hurt. I could have been angry for a long time. Intuitively, I knew that anger was potentially very dangerous. I had to keep in control.

Over those last few months and after the divorce decision, I would go to the café, take my paperwork and do my calculations there etc. It felt good. I was out of the house.

I saw a lawyer. We were still living in the same house,

sleeping in the same bed. I tried the thin mattress on the floor downstairs and decided I did not want back trouble as well as everything else.

He worked from home and refused to move out. How could he? It was his office.

He worked from home, didn't he? We all needed his money, didn't we? He worked from home. End of story.

So I was jumping between: How can I get him out? Where is best place for the three of us to live?

I told him he needed a lawyer. A day later, we were sitting in the lounge when he answered the phone and said to a mutual friend, 'Yes, thanks for your advice. Susan got him first.'

The recommended lawyer in the area.

I told my husband I was going to tell his family why we were divorcing. He was furious. When he was detoxing earlier in the year, he just wanted it kept between the four of us, our dirty little secret. I went along with that. I wanted him to recover so, fair enough.

He certainly did not want me to tell his family the reason we were divorcing. I was having none of that. His family had been my second family for thirty years. I loved these people and I wanted them to know why I was 'throwing in the towel.'

Human behaviour is an amazing thing. Here's an example:

After I came back from my Paris respite in June of 2002 and he had started drinking again, his mother was due to visit. He hadn't been drinking in the house since his relapse. I refused to allow it. He went to pick her up and as soon as she went upstairs to unpack, he poured himself a glass of whisky, brought it into the lounge and sat down in front of the kids and me.

I don't know what his mother thought was going on but I had a fit. The children and I were supposed to watch him behave in a way he thought he might get away with. His mother would not be surprised to see him with a drink at 6 o'clock at night. This was his chance.

I was furious, livid, and threatened to go upstairs and tell her. I poured it down the sink. The children and I were horribly distressed. Me – because I was living with a twat, the children – because mummy and daddy were at it again and now Granny was witnessing it.

We humans are the only species who work with revenge and payback. Apparently, no other animals, birds, behave in this way.

Gosh! Anger and revenge. Hugely powerful, vile, and very bad for the individual. It only keeps the person in a low, low vibrational space.

When I began divorce proceedings I wasn't vengeful; however I was determined to receive a good deal from the divorce. I did carry that thought. I took a friend with me to the meeting with the lawyer. She took notes! I took the valium. Actually I have no recollection if I did take a valium. I'd been to the doctor the day before, reported what was happening in our marriage and sadly, she said again, 'Not you two as well!' When I said I needed a prescription she assumed I had come in for anti-depressants.

I said, 'No, a couple of valium please, because I am so

nervous.' As I said, I can't remember if I actually took a pill. I don't think I did because I had to lead the school choir that evening for the Christmas play! It is absolutely amazing what people do when they put on a front and pretend that their life has not cartwheeled out of control.

Of course, it's probably just the fact that we have other responsibilities which can then help us through the quagmire of shit.

The lawyer asked if I only wanted to pay half up front.

I said, 'No, I've wasted a long time getting here, let's get it done. I'm not going back now!'

I suppose it's a little like writing this book. Get it done. It remains to be seen if this will be cathartic. Many have said that it will, so …

I want the book to be beneficial to others. At the time of preparing this part of the book, I had a physiotherapist session booked. A trapped nerve in my right elbow.

For someone like me who suggests the possibility to clients that their physical pain may be psychosomatic – a result of their emotional pain, then what message should I be receiving?

For me, they were possible signs from the Universe!

Stop this writing now! You knew it was a bad idea. Who are you to think this will benefit anyone?

OR

Slow down, take more time AND get it right!

I chose the second message!

As I wrote and worked on this first edit I can tell you that 'a magical shift' certainly appeared to have taken place I'll let you know what it is towards the end of the book.

However, I have digressed.

I returned home from the lawyers and told my husband that the divorce was now set in place.

In the evening after the school concert, he asked if I would collect him from the pub. It was my local too, so I did. Not a lot of chat there when I arrived. Just his mates trying to make some uneasy conversation.

A few days later, as I dropped my daughter off at the pub for her weekend glass collecting job, I spoke to the landlord's wife. I asked her, 'what's the gossip?' She said what I was expecting to hear.

'It's you two!'

We burst out laughing.

When I think how our life revolved round the pub, I can feel very uneasy.

Before this divorce stage, I had hoped that the pub landlord or his friends would have had tough words with him about his drinking levels. That again with hindsight, was a ridiculous hope. Everyone just wants to protect his or her own little world, be it personal or business related.

Those who have lived with a heavy drinker, an alcoholic,

call it what you will, know the story. Alcohol dependent people drink in a different number of pubs and buy their stocks from a variety of shops.

It was two days after telling my husband I had been to the lawyer, that he stayed in bed threatening suicide – a pathetic heap feeling sorry for himself. He had nothing to live for –I was taking it all away.

I had expected this. I was having none of it. I told the fucker that I was phoning the doctor and she would probably take him to *the said* nuthouse.

He looked a bit surprised. I felt fury and disgust. In a situation like this, those who are not strong enough to live decently and properly can bully people into submission. I was angry. I could see the manipulation.

My, my! Obviously some **anger** still to deal with. I have a YouTube Tapping routine on anger at:

www.youtube.com/watch?v=znqtWgKiWSk

I also have a CD with tapping routines specific to fear, anger, hurt, stress and anxiety emotions.

I would not be able to work professionally with alcoholics. It is too painful, AND, very difficult to achieve success. Usually 'their hand is not up' to work on achieving success. I have moved on. Yes, I have knowledge and understanding but I rather choose to guide people to rediscover their inner confidence when:

they have been tested by an alcoholic

stressed or wounded with divorce

challenged by life after the death of a loved one.

My true passion is working with someone who wishes to find Joy and Purpose in their life and desires the confidence to live it to the full.

www.therealconfidenceguide.com

Life is too short, too short for so many things. Be brave enough to live for yourself first.

Back to the 'lying in bed, waiting for the doctor episode' ...

The doctor came and my husband promised to detox again after the New Year. This was December 12th, or close to that date. The doctor and his original detox therapist who worked with him earlier in the year, were both at the house.

I seem to remember them looking at me to see if I would agree to give him another chance, regardless of the fact that I had a lawyer now acting on my behalf.

I phoned the lawyer and embarrassingly asked him if he would place everything on hold, as my husband was going to detox again. I said to the lawyer's receptionist, without wanting an answer, that I wondered how many times this happens with idiots like me, i.e. delaying an inevitable completion to a truly shite situation.

So many people wanted him to have that second chance. Fucking hell, when I think – another fucking chance! Those who have lived with alcoholics and understand the power of this illness, knows that it is not in anyone's best interests to stay 'on the sinking ship'. It often is a no win situation. The selfish manipulation of the alcoholic means that it is just a form of self-punishment to stay.

I imagine the children were pleased. My daughter read my first edit; I found this encouraging. My son hopes to ignore it all. I knew their father, loved them, although towards the end of our marriage it was difficult to give that thought too much strength and credibility.

The beliefs that children and adults have, and judgements that they may make throughout their lives, are hugely determined by the lessons they learn whilst growing up.

I also believe that a huge number of us try to do the very best for our children. My children were always my concern. However, I doubt that any worry about their reaction to this project would have stopped me from writing this book.

I will assume we were the only important things in his life, but the illness had taken its vice-like grip and he was not the person we loved or had loved. To the rest of our little world, outside the house, he was just a person whose marriage was breaking down. They knew nothing else really. He was still pleasant to them. We took the pain.

After giving him a second chance and some positivity had come back into his space, I overheard him telling his mother what he was buying me for Christmas. I feel sure he broke his mother's heart later on when she realised certain things, but I deviate. He said he was buying me a Christmas present that would blow me away. An eternity ring!

I was gobsmacked. I expect I was gobsmacked because my heart was not in this struggle any more. I was certainly not gobsmacked with delight.

He had agreed with the doctor and his detox lady that he would stop drinking again after the New Year. It seemed a realistic time to start as this was the festive season – a truly magnificent reason for procrastination.

We survived Christmas and on Boxing Day, we laughed at the absurdity of the eternity ring. In the short time between Christmas and the end of the year, I really felt that I did not want to spend New Year celebrations with him. I tried to get out of it. Even so, we went to the pub and spent the evening together – but apart.

Months after I was shown a photograph taken that evening. It showed our group socialising. Everyone was normal except my husband. He was enveloped in a ghostly, spiky and malevolent vice-like grip. Chilling for some perhaps. Puzzling and a shrug of the shoulders from me and the children. The photographer had had the photograph examined by experts. No one had tampered with the it but no explanation could be found. Now that I know more about the 'woo woo world' - the Energy and psychic world, my mind is open to what others may call 'a load of rubbish.'

As part of my terms to try again with our relationship, I insisted that he get office space and work away from home. This was the only way I could contemplate trying to make things work.

In February two days before starting work in his new office the children and I had to endure Roy Orbison's, 'It's Over', put on repeat play. It was obviously a reluctant move. Realisation must have been creeping into his head. He was unhappy, resigned and probably annoyed about detoxing. I was happy and relieved. It was good for me and the children and could have been so good for him.

During these last few months, there were two outbursts of

physical violence. In our marital break-up, physical violence was not an issue. However, there were two occasions when I reacted physically.

He flaunted an association with another woman he had met during the previous six months. This was an attempt to make me jealous.

He would goad me. The kids found texts every now and then on his phone and felt the need to tell me. I assured them I did not want to know. They seemed to think I needed to know. They were teenagers at the time.

On one occasion late in the evening, he wound me up until I lost it and kicked out at him. I missed, and only hurt myself. I had pulled a muscle or something. My daughter accompanied me to the hospital. I came back with crutches.

At this point, the school knew I was going through a divorce so I don't know what anyone thought. I simply said that I had hurt myself.

When there is emotional distress causing havoc it can lead to physical distress and illness. Physical injuries can be a result of emotional weakness held in the body. A specific area in the body can be weakened and therefore damaged more easily, should emotional distress be high. This is a simplistic explanation but nevertheless, strongly accepted by those working in the field of emotional well-being.

Not long after the crutches affair he again goaded me intently. My daughter and I were on the sofa and he came across to me, very close. I raised my feet, placed them on his belly and booted him across the floor.

My daughter just screamed and ordered me to go to a friend's house – to clear off. He lay grumbling on the floor.

I came back the next morning and it was as normal. Nothing was said.

Chapter 8
The end – as dramatic as it gets

After New Year and his second go at detoxing, moving out of the house and into his office, things took a further downturn.

I think I tried to be supportive. To be honest I wanted him to work out of the house and I knew this would potentially make things easier should the lawyer need to retrieve the divorce papers from the back drawer.

I was completely focused on myself, the children and the rules that had been set in place when I agreed to give him his second chance.

I assume, (something I do not recommend) that he found his life deeply stressful at that stage – falling apart, or certainly changing.

He started drinking again fairly quickly after the second attempted detox.

Things deteriorated fast.

There was a woman he was texting. The children helped me with that one. I could not get it through to them that I did not want to know all the grubby details. I knew enough and maybe deep down I did not want to become angry. As I said, this was not a physically abusive relationship and I did not want to be the one who instigated that. I imagine that he may have wanted this to happen, as some form of leverage for him, should I actually continue with divorce.

I read some of the texts but didn't really care less. I did some detective work and found out that she was associated with a dubious massage house. In my head, that was just another thing to add to the list of items constituting irretrievable breakdown of marriage.

We had lunch late on Sunday afternoons. This was unpleasant for many Sundays. I would tape record those meals. The kids knew I did this. I did not try to lead the conversation: neither did they. We did not egg him on. Sadly, I had discussions with them about how messy their parents' relationship was. We were not getting anywhere so I had to acquire evidence in order to get best deal for the three of us.

I rarely do Sunday lunch now. At the time it was:

- We came back from the pub.
- I did not go to the pub much then but had to go to collect my daughter who worked there. I did not want her in the car with him when he drove back.
- He would then listen to U2 with earphones on.
- We ate.
- We had to put up with a build-up of his anger when he came to the table.

Miserable times.

During the two years prior to this, I found out that my son rarely brought friends over at the weekends. I could write so much more but I want to avoid a list of deeply embarrassing incidents. One of my children mentioned to me a bit later that they were just waiting for another year because they would be finished school and be able to leave home. Get out of the ' warring parents' home.

My son asked me, 'What can you do to sort Dad out?'

I said that there was nothing more I could think of doing. They thought Mum could wave the magic wand. Unfortunately, the wand had run out of fairy dust.

There is no mileage raking it all up but what a mess parents inflict on their children by trying to do the right thing. I'm talking about me here. I needed to get my husband out of the house. He had me over a barrel. Months passed and the children had to put up with it all.

So many people try to brush their problems under the carpet. Is it a British thing? If so, what a right bunch we are!

Please feel free to comment on my book website.

www.surviveandthriveaftertruma.com

When someone is under the influence of drink and when someone drinks even more in the belief that it helps them to deal with life's issues, you are no longer working, living or dealing with a safe and rational person.

Why I stayed so long is a bit of a mystery but I can say that I now believe the Universe does indeed work in mysterious ways.

Over a period of eighteen months, my daughter challenged him about his hidden bottles. She waved them in his face. He ignored it or was verbally abusive to her.

Fortunately, my sister had seen him the year before, at his worst, and before the first detox. It was Hogmanay in Edinburgh on Princes Street. She heard how he spoke to our daughter as we wove our way through the masses, holding on to each other to avoid being separated. It is very easy to lose each other in Edinburgh's Princes Street on New Year's Eve!

He was verbally very abusive to her. She was only fourteen. When my sister displayed her shock to us, my daughter and I just looked at each other. This abuse had been going on for such a while that it had become second nature.

It was comforting that my sister had witnessed some of this nasty behaviour; seen what happened when he was fuelled with alcohol. Because she was my sister I suspect she had thoughts of 'it takes two to spoil a marriage.' She hadn't interfered with our mess and had only been a quiet sounding board for me when I would lament about 'what to do?' I suspect, as my older sister she considered me to be opinionated, lacking some tolerance, outspoken when defensive. I prefer to consider myself as spirited! Some months after that evening when the going was getting really tough, I escaped for the weekend and he unexpectedly telephoned her. He discussed our marriage at length and asked if she was prepared to have some sympathy towards his side of things. She told him her loyalties lay with me. His behaviour on New Year's Eve reinforced any doubt she had. He never spoke to her again.

In February, I phoned the lawyer and said, 'Please continue with the divorce proceedings.'

I was going up to Scotland for a few days' break and the divorce papers arrived the day I was leaving. The lawyer hadn't dawdled on this.

During these last few months I also had to tolerate my husband bombarding me with awful texts when I went out with friends. Abusive texts. He did this regularly. These friends were also his friends. I would show them the texts and receive a puzzled look or comment such as: 'Why is he doing this?'

I write this to further highlight the emotionally sick and misguided way an alcoholic will behave. It is the fuel of the alcohol that gives someone a misguided bravery, feeding an inadequacy deep in the psyche.

No one, man or woman should put up with this kind of behaviour.

In relation to my husband moving out, I asked my son if he was staying with me. He was seventeen at the time. He looked at me and said, 'Mum I don't know where or what I'm going to do. Dad says I can stay with him too.' This was a disappointment but hardly a surprise. Confusion reigned.

Incidentally, I was aware that there was this masseuse woman involved in whatever arrangement was taking place. They were going to share what was actually a very nice flat.

He would live there in the evening and work in his office during the day. She would have her clients there during the day. Her clients were not there for a manicure! I later met this woman. I liked her. She bought me lunch.

After the incident of my booting him across the floor, one of my girlfriends invited me to dinner. She picked me up and I got a taxi home. This also happened to be four days before he was moving out of the house – for good. The nasty texts arrived. The evening ended and I returned home.

I peeked into the lounge and saw he was lying on the floor

with the headphones on, listening to U2. I went into the kitchen, took off my wedding ring: I did not want to wear it anymore. Time to move on.

My daughter spoke briefly to me along the lines of: 'Dad pissed me off and we fell out.'

I found out later that my son had said unpleasant stuff to him too. Awful sickening memories.

I went up to the bedroom. My sister had strongly suggested that we sleep in separate beds by now. We didn't. Over the year I realised that it was always going to be me who slept on the teeny foldaway mattress and me who was going to get the sore back. So we still shared the bed.

As I lay in bed I was thinking, 'Gosh this is it.' and then my mind turned to 'I won't get a shag in a hurry.'

I was still awake when he came in. I suggested sex. I hadn't had it in six months. At this point niceties didn't play a part in our relationship, needless to say. I won't soften the words that were in my thought process. He came to bed. He agreed. It wasn't anything other than a sad ending but it was done. No nastiness. Just done.

I don't really know what I was thinking afterwards. But I got out of bed and then he said he wasn't feeling well. I remember him saying, 'this isn't good. I really don't feel well.' I said I would get him a drink of water. That's my stock answer to everything when someone is not feeling 100%. 'Have a drink and go to the toilet!'

He was sweating profusely. Serious sweating. I said I would get a bucket for him in case he was sick. I rushed to fetch it from the bathroom. He was grey and sweating all over his body so I was not surprised when he started vomiting. I went downstairs to get him a drink of water.

My memory is very clear about what happened next. So to indulge myself, to cleanse myself, I will continue.

I went downstairs and thought I'd tuck into some houmous and pitta bread. I heard a thud.

I thought I'd better go upstairs. I took the water and found him sitting on the end of the bed, totally collapsed over his legs, but supported somehow. I knew instinctively that something was very wrong. He was grey and unconscious. I screamed loudly for the children to come through and help. I rolled him on the bed, screaming, and tried CPR but the bed was soft and there was no purchase. When my daughter came in I screamed at her to call an ambulance. My son eventually came in. It was 2 o'clock in the morning. Although we did not make a habit of rowing in bed, my son later said he thought I was screaming because we were having an argument.

My son and I got him off the bed. My daughter was on the phone speaking to the 999 - emergency services - person relaying to me what I should be doing, regarding mouth-to-mouth resuscitation.

My son helped me. They can say what they like about CPR and artificial respiration, but when you are in a blind panic, completely and emotionally involved with the situation, trying to do it correctly can go right out the window. I realised that I wasn't holding his nose. I was getting nowhere. The paramedics arrived very quickly. My daughter had done a great job, as had my son.

Why did I write in such detail? Possibly to explain how many of us react to trauma. All the very small detail when replayed over and over in our thought process, will only gain strength when tucked away in the subconscious. But these horrible small details are part of the past. They are not a prerequisite for the future. Somehow they must be released or cleared. That is why my work and learning is now EFT, Matrix Reimprinting and Mindset behaviour.

It was a chapter in my life. That is all. It was a chapter for our children.It was his final chapter.

The paramedics worked on him for twenty minutes. I remember my daughter and I went out of the bedroom, probably to get them a drink. We were in shock. My son was still in there. We could not get back in and my son later said that as he was holding his father's head while the paramedics administered adrenalin and used defibrillation treatment all he could see was his father's face getting bluer and bluer.

At no point during the resuscitation attempt by the paramedics did the children or I consider the fact that my husband their father, was dead. I remember being somewhat puzzled that they brought him downstairs on an ambulance trolley, put him outside the front door, and left him for a few minutes while they went back upstairs and tidied up. This was 3 a.m. in the morning, in March. He was on the trolley with no cover. My brain just would not take it in.

When we drove off shortly after the ambulance I told the children that I didn't think he was going to make it. My son said the doctors would be able to sort him out.

Once in the hospital waiting room a young doctor came

and told us that my husband had died. I feel sure it was his first time! He did a good enough job of it. The nurse asked if we wanted to say goodbye.

We went in. Gosh, a dead body is a dead body. Lifeless. What else can you say?

In hindsight, he was already dead when I went back upstairs, carrying his water. However you look at this, when the spirit leaves the body, when the spirit has gone, only an empty shell is left – a husk. That is all. The spirit has flown and is elsewhere.

I asked the children to kiss their father goodbye. They were not keen but I urged them to do so as they might well regret not doing so at some later point in their lives. A little reluctantly they did. I did too. I just felt I was shaking my head quietly and slowly for a long time that night, trying to figure it all out.

The friend I'd been with that evening arrived later.

Again a nurse came in to the waiting room and asked if I wanted to come and take his wedding ring and chain. I went in alone with the nurse. I looked at his body and just shook my head saying, 'God, what a fool. What a fool.'

My feelings were of disbelief, resignation, tiredness, and what a waste of a life.

I have to say that years later, a couple of brave people did suggest other things, one being: 'My my, weren't you let off the hook!'

I was let off the hook. Maybe I was *deserving* of some good.

Later that day our family doctor arrived to give her condolences. She too was surprised by his death. She asked if I or the children had heard him complaining about chest pain at any point before. None of us had. The fact remained that he would probably not have visited the doctor because she would have called his attention to the drinking.

The life-threatening seriously blocked arteries which were the reason for his death were not discovered. We were both smokers. He had been very stressed, a heavy drinker of alcohol, and took no exercise. He was an intelligent man and was surely watching his life fall apart. Enormous stress factors.

A couple of our very close friends helped me with some of the funeral arrangements. The funeral was very well attended and I read the eulogy. It was not an issue. It was my decision, my idea and a perfectly natural thing for me to consider doing. We had been together since 1973 – a long time – thirty years.

We'd had; a lot of good times, a lot of life, some completely hellish times.

But I owed him for the good times, and our children.

Chapter 9
Epilogue

On the morning after the funeral I wakened to a beautiful sunny morning. I felt as if a weight had been lifted from my shoulders. I unquestionably felt a feeling of freedom.

I was aware, and still am aware, that I had probably been let off the hook by my husband's death. The stress I had been under and how it might affect me physically, was something I intuitively seemed to understand.

I felt a freedom and relief. I really believe I never felt guilt about his death. I was stunned and shocked. The counsellors and one or two friends asked me if I felt any guilt. One friend spoke very seriously to me that I should not feel guilt because the state of his arteries meant he could have died by just climbing the stairs. Guilt about his death? No. I did my very best until I knew I needed out to save my sanity and health. I had made the choice and I chose me. Perhaps in that respect I had feelings of guilt but even so, I am not sure how much if any guilt I felt. It was just awful that someone had to die.

His death released our two children and me from his needy mess. However, no one gets off scot-free. When I consider my feelings deeply I am aware I still have some remaining anger issues. There is also a fundamental sadness. My children do not have their father. That was the area I had to work with: to forgive him for the fact that his children were not enough to keep him healthier or alive.

A great future learning for me was that I understood and realised that I did not have to be responsible for him during his life. I was not his mother. In life we often take on roles.

Once you are seen in a particular role it is a little tricky to remove yourself should you decide you don't want that role any more.

I have so much I still want to learn. I am no braver than many but I actively *press the button,* gasp and wonder expectantly how it will all work out. I especially remember doing that when pressing the button on Online Dating. That was fun!

On the back of my car I have a sticker: 'Enjoy Life's Journey.'

I urge you to enjoy your journey. We only have an allocated time here on earth. Don't waste it.

I suggest to you if something in your personal or business life is not working – change it. The answer does not need to be massively transformational. Tweaks, talking, sharing and *clear the bloody fear for God's sake* may be all that needs to happen. However, big hard changes are necessary at times.

Some may need a harsh, authentic message.

Get off your arse and start improving your life. When you sense a glimmer, a *sign* that tells you to deal with your issues, to improve your life, then

'Just Do It'.

Chapter 10
Discovering EFT and 'Working in the Light'

'When one door closes another door opens, but we so often look so long and so regretfully upon the closed door, that we do not see the ones which open for us.'
Alexander Graham Bell

'Working in the Light'

During training in a Matrix Reimprinting Advanced Tools workshop I asked to be a guinea pig and to work with one of the trainers.

The lessons I learned I accept quite rationally. I only wish I had started working in the field of Energy Psychology much earlier in my life. However, I needed to be led into it. I find the work I do fascinating.

Ortal Peleg and Sasha Allenby were running this course. I worked with Ortal.

We started with EFT and some tapping to quieten down to tune in to one another.

The issue: My husband's death. The part I'd only ever shared with a very few people: the sex before his death.

I was asked to take my issue to *The Light;* to a place of peace and clarity where lessons can be learned and better understood.

Where is that? It is where you want it to be. Some people find a place quickly, others take a little time.

I could not find a place of light or perhaps a place of peace.

There was too much mental interference: my thoughts, pictures, people were getting in the way.

Certainly not a clear place. I took it up into the sky – still not good enough – still too much interference.

I worked on it and took it up into the sky, into the vast universe, but still had difficulty in finding a clear space to acquire any learning. I suppose that shows the degree to which my subconscious was getting in my way. Someone may comment and tell me their thoughts, online. I write later about 'Secondary Gain'. I fear I had some of those!

So I found myself going back to *The Big Bang* – the time when time began – a place free from all possible interference.

I had a fantastic few moments. I saw myself bouncing through time, no barriers One moment in one place, another moment, God knows where – a free spirit. From one part of the Universe to another – in a moment. Not a problem, not an issue.

The learning I chose to take was that I was not responsible for anything other than me. I was not responsible for his life or how he chose to live it. That had been his choice.

His life was his. I was a part of his life here on earth. His spirit in that body was finished. It was time for him to leave this terrestrial plane. Goodness knows why he came into his body and what his journey in this life was to learn. I realised that his time was over.

As for me, I realised I still had a life to lead. That satisfied me. His time was over. Mine wasn't.

I wondered whether it was time to let go or hold on.

In my case I had had a good excuse to *not let go* completely. I had two children who I hope will be able to remember the good times.

When you are dealing with the grief, anger, or the unfairness of any trauma and you have children who are part of that scenario, then it is not unusual for lots of discussion, and reassurance to continue. Many conversations between the children and I took place. It is a constant reminder.

Time has to be an answer here. We were all horrified. In my case, the divorce was a death to me. I was closed emotionally so I seemed to be stunned by my husband's death but not grief-stricken. I may also have been grateful on a subconscious level; I was most definitely stunned. In time I realised that it is the remembering of the good parts that is beneficial, cleansing and therapeutic.

I reflect on the fact that his time was up. I take comfort that his last moments here on earth perhaps left him with a feeling that he wasn't so bad – so alone. He was not alone when he died and surely, that is most fortunate for me and our children. Goodness only knows! I choose to hold that belief and therefore it can help me continue with *my journey*.

The *Sliding Doors* scenario. He could have moved out, died alone. Plenty of room for guilt with that ending.

On the morning of his death, I received a letter from his lawyer asking if I would give him another six months to sort himself out ('to dry out'). Would I put everything on hold? In other words, give him another chance.

I pondered a little over this as you can imagine and what I

believe is that I would have divorced him. I had had enough.

The *Sliding Doors* scenario again. I am 100% certain I would have received no peace for a considerable amount of time had he left and stayed in his unhappy state. I would now be different, possibly deeply troubled. I am eternally grateful that my children are wonderful, decent young people and I will leave it there.

The phrase 'let off the hook' seems apt so I embrace that, say a thank you up to the Universe and enjoy the times when all is good. I ask you, Which door do *you* open?

It's a 'no brainer' surely. Do yourself a favour. The door you believe will lead to opportunity is the door to open.

If you are in that position, open the correct door. The Law of Attraction can then be helpful because you are attracting positive energy. If we feel, believe and know that we deserve good things, the choice is easy.

We now move onto Section 2 - Resources, then Section 3 - Contributions.

These sections are informative for those who wish to understand more about emotions and to find tools and methods to help troubled emotions. The accounts in Section 3 are from those who are thriving after their challenges. You may appreciate the messages they share.

Section 2
Resources to help Emotional Healing
with explanations for a deeper understanding of emotive terminology and emotive conditions

Words emboldened earlier in the book are now given deeper explanation. I may give my interpretation and direct you to the advantages of EFT and Matrix Reimprinting therapy.

In some sections, I have included:

- an occasional personal experience
- questions for you to consider
- Clean Language questions for deeper resolution.

A Clean Language question is a simple clarifying question which enables the person who creates the problem to solve it. Clean Language was devised by David Grove, a counselling psychologist.

A couple of years after my husband died I learned tools and techniques to help me relieve stress and anxiety. I start with the techniques I favour when working with a client: EFT and Matrix Reimprinting.

Emotional Freedom Techniques® (EFT)

EFT is a strategy used to address emotional distress.

We tap on energy meridians in the body whilst focussing on the relevant distress issue.eg

I am so distressed when I consider the helplessness of my given situation that I cannot breathe or function properly anymore.

We aim to lower the stress and anxiety held in the body. Emotional distress results in physical distress and can lead to disease and sickness.

An ever increasing number of Counsellors and Hypnotherapists use EFT to create shifts in clients before they continue their chosen route of treatment. Some EFTers question the need to follow a different route. We believe we can achieve speedy and effective results with EFT based therapy.

I guide someone to take a new perspective on what they can achieve in Life's Abundance. Abundance in Health, Wealth, Happiness and Success.

I have loved learning about releasing negative, limiting beliefs and emotions. I believe very strongly that no one need live their life by someone else's persuasion; however quietly and insidiously it has been drip fed into their life.

Find my EFT tapping resources and YouTube videos, showing tapping for fear and anger, on my website.

www.hampshire-eft.co.uk

Matrix Reimprinting

Matrix Reimprinting is a development of EFT. We work with 'echoes' from our younger self. We can Reimprint a positive outcome to a past trauma. We can Reimprint to our future self: we can see ourselves as successful, fulfilled, more content. If you are someone who recognises that you are 'holding onto trauma' then this therapy and the positive visualisation can be very beneficial to you.

A key statement:

> The subconscious does not know what is right or wrong, true or false. This is fundamental to understanding the power of the subconscious which is only trying to keep us safe.

With that in mind, please consider an old belief or memory that has been stored in your subconscious. You may give it power by allowing it to dictate your thoughts, e.g.

- I can't sit under a tree because I might see a spider.
- I won't ask that awful boss of mine for help. He's just like my father.
- If I tell a lie my nose will grow.

Can you begin to see how ridiculous it is to live by these old beliefs?

I base my practitioner work on EFT and Matrix Reimprinting and therefore I help people to heal themselves.

Stress management is greatly eased with EFT but I believe it is the deeper Matrix Reimprinting when working at deep, core level, which is truly beneficial. Otherwise, the root cause is still there waiting to trip you up another time.

www.therealconfidenceguide.com

The real confidence guide is my niche site, directed mainly at women. Women are much more proactive when wanting to change a confidence, self-esteem or self-belief issue. When you are confident life appears easier.

One of my **bonuses** is an article on Matrix Reimprinting by **Karl Dawson** which you can download from:

www.surviveandthriveaftertrauma.com

The article explains this process very well. It should. Karl is the creator of Matrix Reimprinting.

Visualisation

Creative visualisation is part of positive thinking.

It is used by those wishing to *see* their goal. It is part of a spiritual exercise; to see it, feel it, hear it, taste it, smell it.

When used with The Law of Attraction it can allow us to move from a negative starting point to attracting a positive outcome.

We can trick our subconscious. As mentioned before, our subconscious does not know what is right or what is wrong.

Severe Trauma

Big T *'Trauma': potentially serious, e.g. sexual abuse, violent assault, being taken hostage, torture – anything that threatens life.*

Small t *'trauma': life events in our younger earlier days which can shatter our life security.*

A small 't' can be highly stressful and deeply traumatic for us if the incident happens unexpectedly and the person is not prepared for it, or if someone is being intentionally cruel. There is a feeling of **Powerlessness** to prevent something happening. That feeling of powerlessness can rear its head at various points later in one's life.

A trauma, if witnessed at under six years of age, when a child is in a hypnogogic state (a very suggestive state), can cause a continuation of the negative learned beliefs to be triggered throughout life when a similar situation or action is experienced.

Over six years of age, our brain develops so that we are not in such a suggestive stage, not so accepting. The principal that all negative beliefs are learned under six years of age is accepted by many in the field of energy psychology. It need not be a big issue just a misinterpreted message.

However, I am discussing my emotional trauma; divorce, alcoholism, continual verbal abuse and death of someone: small 't' trauma. Emotions of anger, fear, sadness, responsibility, hopelessness, rage, being used and abused, loss, useless. These are certainly not life-threatening though.

Most of the contributions included in Section 3 are small 't' trauma. A couple of my contributors discuss big 'T' Trauma.

Question: Is a traumatic event in your life causing you to feel restricted or quite simply does it dictate the person you are now, today?

Can you consider that the event happened, it was totally ghastly but life goes on?

Clean question: If so, what do you want to have happen? And what needs to happen for that to happen?

Bonus Click on the link to my website for the 'EFT Tap for Trauma' routine. www.surviveandthriveaftertrauma.com

You can change the word 'trauma' to a word of your choice. One of these downloadable tapping sheets is titled 'Tapping Points (all points) detailing benefits.' With this information, you can instantly find the point which can be of most benefit to you and use it discreetly in any stressful situation.

If you wish to work on severe trauma, it is important to work with a trained practitioner.

Heart Math Breathing

Heart Math Breathing is a temporary fix which can be used when in a panic attack or high state of anxiety.

Here is how it works.

- We keep ourselves centred.
- We keep ourselves focused, in the present.
- We put our hands on our heart.
- Feet firmly planted on the floor.
- Close our eyes.
- Breathe in for a count of six, focusing on the heart
- Breathe out, from the heart, for a count of six.

If we can do that four or five times for a couple of minutes, it has a wonderfully calming effect.

Secondary Gain (SG)

A Secondary Gain can be defined as an indirect benefit when someone unconsciously (or consciously) gains more attention, or sympathy from others.

I love this section. From being a primary teacher for more than thirty years and going into the world of psychotherapy, when I understood secondary gain, I was fascinated. I had had no reason to think or read about SG, but when I understood one of mine, it blew me away. Perhaps I am an innocent, a genuine person, unselfish, not a manipulator or an emotional blackmailer. It is probable that the majority of people who manipulate or carry the benefits of SG. are unaware of what they are actually doing.

Two years before my twenty-fifth wedding anniversary when I was talking to my doctor I was unaware that I was harbouring a SG. I was living within a possibly unsteady marriage but I believed I deserved a bloody good holiday for achieving twenty-five years. And I had no intention of missing out on that.

Here is a short list which may help you to better understand a secondary gain. I keep many explanations simple. No offence is meant.

1. Someone moderately unwell. They are unable to do chores, take on a job, bring in financial contribution. Perhaps the very thought of the lifestyle change needed to release the secondary gain is just too large to consider. The individual therefore maintains the SG scenario because if they do become physically or mentally stronger, presumably they will be expected to start contributing in the areas which were previously

undertaken by others.

2. The angry person, possibly justified in their anger. Perhaps holding on to that anger gives reason or excuse for a particular behaviour.

3. The person who doesn't pull their weight in a team at work. They know someone else will cover for them. Perhaps their good excuse is just a cover for inadequacy.

If the true reason is actually a SG for that individual, then in time they may soon be discovered. But sometimes it is almost impossible for an individual to see that there is a SG taking place. It needs discovering or is discovered through therapy, counselling etc.

People can become most upset if challenged into considering this explanation. The realisation can be really frightening: effort would be needed to change.

However, if you are in a position to start rectifying a given situation, the growth, the self-satisfaction, the confidence, the improvement in your life and to those around you, is colossal.

When I was writing this, I saw a great comment written in Facebook along the lines of:

'Victims are so often controllers and knowingly or unknowingly, they use being a victim to control others.'

Susan's Secondary Gain
probably not my only one!

I include this as an example to help explain a SG.

I was learning Matrix Reimprinting and my trainer was the wonderful Ted Wilmont. I have used artistic licence here and have incorporated two separate learning opportunities through which I understood a substantial SG.

Scenario: Ted listening to his students who are practising with each other:

I was attempting to release my thoughts, ties and the ghastliness around my husband's death. The numbers mentioned relate to the number of intensity of the distress I was feeling. A one is a very low stress level and ten is the highest number of the stress intensity.

Me: Well, I can get my number down to a number one. I've tried to clear it and can't. But a one is fine. It's OK.

Ted (interrupting): OK, Susan, why can't you just get it go down to zero? Why can't you let it go?

Me: I don't know. Ask me again.

Ted: Susan, why can't you let it go? Get it to a zero?

Me (raising my voice): I don't know! Ask me again!

Ted: Susan, why can't you just let it go?

Me (shouting): I don't know! I don't know! I don't know (shrugging).

Realisation –   Well bugger me!

Bloody Hell!   I don't deserve to let it go.

I need to punish myself!

And also … If I let it go, I will not have my husband to blame – to blame when I feel angry. After all, poor me, look what I went through!

I have an excuse.

If I do not have that excuse then I am responsible for my behaviour (ah, no thanks!). Then I can't blame him. I am responsible. I can't hide any more behind my wonderful excuse.

But the excuse is only an excuse. Only in my eyes because: *'There are none so blind as those who will not see.'*

I laughed or smiled with disbelief when I realised what was holding me back. It is very interesting and fantastic when it shines out at you. I love it when clients have their 'light bulb moment'.

Question: Can you recognise an area in your life where you think you may harbour a S.G.?

Clean question: What would you like to have happen? What needs to happen for that to happen?

Reiki

Reiki is a Japanese word made up of two syllables.

REI means 'aura' or 'spiritual consciousness'.

KI means 'energy' or 'power' – the 'life force'.

Think of it as spiritually guided life force energy.

Reiki is a hands-on healing method used to channel this energy.

I believe Reiki has helped to keep me emotionally and physically healthy. I believe it has a wondrous effect on stress levels.

Many people enjoy, benefit and heal with Reiki.

My gorgeous cat George used to come to me for Reiki. Lucy my beautiful tabby cat did not seem to require it.

I am a Reiki 3 practitioner. My small website is

www.susancowereiki.com

Counselling

Please note: I have counselling skills but am not an Accredited Counsellor.

Counselling can help emotional healing. It is mainstream and recognised by the masses.

There are different schools of thought around counselling. Different approaches. eg. Cognitive Behavioural Therapy (CBT), Person Centred Counselling, Gestalt Counselling, Psychoanalytic Therapy.

I had Cruse Counselling; bereavement counselling. It lasted six months. I started it about a year after my husband's death. I enjoyed it and the 'offloading' made me feel better. My counsellor said I was the best birthday present she had received.

I then studied Levels 1, 2 and 3 of Person Centred Counselling. I was drawn to find some understanding around the crap I had gone through. I thought perhaps I could help others at a later point.

During this time I was slowly allowing myself to feel less self-protecting. However I definitely was aware of becoming emotionally vulnerable. I was open to 'feeling' again. As a result, four years after the Cruse sessions I was offered more counselling from my doctor. I had been 'blocking' the effect of the trauma and more regurgitation was required. After six weeks of CBT, the counsellor asked if I wanted a further six sessions. She felt I may benefit!

I did benefit but with regard to counselling and the long time it takes for the individual to find their own answers, I certainly had no desire to find employment in that field. I understand why people '*don't want to go there again'*.

Once I understood the power of EFT and Matrix therapy which gives an opportunity to deflate the stress, take the power out of the anxiety and to clear blocks to resolution much quicker, then to me I'd found what I was looking for.(I also enjoy a bit of U2)

However as a result of having more counselling, I believe:

- I did not love him at the end.
- I probably kept from losing my temper during the final stages of our marriage because I realised subconsciously, that I may have done something awful and the children had suffered enough. They did not need their mother in jail.

The jury is out over that. Perhaps I exaggerate.

Very recently I volunteered to read Maxine Harley's book titled: 'The Ripple Effect' Process. Maxine has a very honest approach. She pulls no punches and explains comprehensively how she maintains that your life can be improved by combining Psycho-Emotional-Education: the 'whole brain' and holistic approach to psychological, emotional and spiritual well-being – not one isolated approach. Should you be interested in a detailed book covering the holistic approach, this is worth a read.

Self-sabotage

'*Self-sabotage is when we say we want something and
then go about making sure it doesn't happen.*'
Alyce P. Cornyn-Selby

I realised at one stage whilst writing this book that I had
forgotten to include self-sabotage. I kept thinking I would
get it done but my book had taken longer than I expected!

- I was tired !

- I had surely done enough!

Perhaps I could just miss out the section on self-sabotage!

The result for me would be that I would have let myself
down in the end. I would have omitted to include a very
important resource and that would have been unfortunate.

I wish to share this :

Self-Sabotage: The Enemy Within[4]

1. *We all get in our own way occasionally and some
   people do it repeatedly, whether it's procrastinating,
   drinking, or overeating. Self-sabotaging behaviour
   results from a misguided attempt to rescue
   ourselves from our own negative feelings.*

---

[4]   http://www.psychologytoday.com/articles/201109/self-sabotage-the-enemy-within

2. *Comfort eating is a common form of self-sabotage, especially when a person has weight concerns; self-medicating with drugs or alcohol is another common form, although procrastination may be the most common of all.*

3. *Addicts, for example, present a parade of excuses and delusional thinking while avoiding the painful, decisive action necessary to set their lives right. All too often, we hear stories of talented individuals who, despite much potential, allowed drugs and alcohol to drag them down. For some, this is fodder for celebrity gossip and tabloid junk. For me, it's the story of my life.*

My husband comes into category 3.

Self-sabotage is clearly linked to procrastination. I will confide that I had an issue regarding which of my surnames I would use as the author of the book. Suffice to say, I procrastinated which meant the potential for self-sabotage was high.

Question: When nearing completion of a project, plan or exciting and worthwhile event, have you 'shot yourself in the foot' and it's all come to nothing?

Clean question: Is there anything else about that?

And now back to a 'dirty' question. Is there a relationship between self-sabotage and a belief that you are not good enough?

Powerlessness

An instinctive response of 'fight' or 'flight' to a threat which may have saved your life but if you "freeze" thereafter, you may have Post Traumatic Stress Disorder(PTSD).

A single event or a pattern in the past is when you have given away your power. Your reaction in a similar challenging situation today, recreates the same feeling of powerlessness within you. It happens subconsciously. You may feel incapable of doing anything. It is a primal trigger, a form of protection.

If you are involved in a 'fight' situation, being beaten physically or emotionally, then you may respond by fight, flight or freeze. If you freeze and close down your responses, you feel as if you are not able to do anything. As a child, perhaps you were unable to fight back; you ran away or froze: If you froze, your body may still be reacting to that trauma today:your body 'numbs out' to protect you from trauma. However, that trauma remains frozen in the subconscious.

It can be released one day by some form of Energy Healing eg EFT to lower the high anxiety followed by Matrix Reimprinting to re-programme the subconscious instilling a positive learning eg.

- I was fearful then but I do not have to remain fearful today.

The Reimprinting of a positive picture can give a triumphant resolution to your past trauma and you carry that forward in life.

Animals release trauma in the moment after it is created. Humans expect or are actively trained to seek comfort in order to feel safe. Consider; 'hush hush it's OK, you will be alright'

If we were able to shake off our trauma on its moment of impact then we would not freeze the moment in our subconscious. And then there would be nothing to replay over and over and over again.

I have included a link to a video of a polar bear naturally releasing its trauma. Watch Karl Dawson, the creator of Matrix Reimprinting explain:

- the bear's natural reaction to releasing its trauma
- and why humans may hold on to trauma.

www.youtube.com/watch?v=8u40WwqkOws

Question: What trigger situation or statement memory makes you feel powerless? Can you think of an earlier memory when you experienced that feeling before?

Clean questions: Does that memory have a taste, shape or colour? Whereabouts do you feel that taste, shape of colour?

What do you want to have happen? What needs to happen for that to happen?

Forgiveness

Forgiveness is letting go of the need for revenge and releasing negative thoughts of bitterness and resentment.

OK, this is a real big one. If you know an unforgiving, bitter or resentful person, you can sense it in every fibre of their being, whether it is a set look on their face, the tone in their voice, or their body is literally showing signs of being bitter and twisted.

My difficulty to forgive was based on this… Our children should have been reason enough for my husband to tidy up his act; to stay alive. His children were the most important people in his life, or so I believed. In that respect, for a while, I equated his death to a form of suicide. I felt anger over that. Or was it pain and hurt?

For a client to consider being able to forgive is key in therapy. Being unable to forgive maintains a deeply held area of pain. To learn to forgive is huge and pivotal for growth transformation. Deep healing from within is necessary.

I have often considered that someone who is unforgiving feels absolutely justified in holding on to and nurturing their negative belief. But … you only remain in your own pain.

On this subject, Nelson Mandela says, *'It's like taking poison and expecting someone else to suffer.'*

Louise Hay says, *'It's like being stuck in a prison of self-righteous resentment.'*

So why keep ourselves in this prison? The person who caused us to feel this way probably forgot about it many moons ago. Yet we still harbour deep resentment.

To be unforgiving is extremely bad for physical, emotional and mental health. The release that is felt with forgiveness is monumental. I include a resource detailing 'The Emotional Scale' which highlights levels of emotion and where we vibrate on the scale. If you are unforgiving, you are basically vibrating moment to moment in the lowest possible state of being.

Frequently when working with a client I show them this resource and ask them to consider where they would place themself on the scale. If they are able to rise one level, it is truly remarkable how many others may also benefit.

Imagine if you are pleasant to someone and the result is that they feel good. They may be more pleasant to someone else ... and so it goes on.

Dr David Hawkins, author of 'Power vs Force: The Hidden Detriments of Human Behaviour', maintains:

'should one person raise their emotional level, it has a positive effect on a very large number of others.'

The refusal to forgive keeps you in a state of unhappiness and damages healthy well-being.

Forgiveness:

- does not require reconciliation with the person who harmed you
- does not mean you condone particular behaviour.

It is about letting go. Being free.

Being unforgiving is indeed a poison and very difficult to

dispel. It is very difficult to make a shift without deep healing work. I recommend Matrix Reimprinting with practitioner guidance.

Question: Do you feel unforgiving toward someone? Is that feeling truly worthwhile for you?

Perhaps a very strong memory holds you in its power. Matrix work is excellent in shifting those destructive beliefs.

Clean Question: Does the inability to forgive have a shape, colour or taste? What needs to happen between forgiving and resolution?

The Emotional Scale

Peace   Bliss   Serenity   Enlightenment   Joy Unconditional-Love   Miracles   Knowledge   Gratitude Appreciation Revelation Laughter Freedom Love Faith
FORGIVENESS Compassion Cleansed Transcendence Passion   Acceptance   Enthusiasm   Eagerness Delighted   Happiness   Optimism   Hopefulness
Positive-Expectation   Belief   Relief   Trust Confidence   Release   Neutrality   Contentment Humility   Courage   Affirmation   Empowerment
Boredom Scorn Pride Dis-contentment Desire Pessimism Frustration   Irritation   Impatience   Agitated
Disappointment   Doubt   Confused   Worry   Scepticism Procrastination   Indecisive   Cynical
Anger Revenge Fear Worry Rage Discouragement Trepidation   Anxiety   Grief
Judgmental Apathy Stuck Resentment Embarrassment Ridicule Despair Rage Racism Prejudice Hostility Blame Guilt Jealousy Competition Sadness Depression Envy
Unworthiness Shame Humiliation Hurt Insecurity Hatred Bitterness   UNFORGIVENESS   Powerless   Hopeless Loneliness   Trauma   Victim

During my Matrix learning, I listened to a Matrix webinar on Forgiveness given by Natasha Abudarham Black. Natasha spoke about her need to forgive.

There may be variations of the Emotional Scale. I am sharing Natasha's.

If we look at the table and believe that we vibrate at the higher end of the scale then we are in good emotional condition. The further down the emotional scale we place ourselves, the poorer our quality of emotional contentment or happiness.

Natasha states that this Scale has been adapted from various sources including Phoenix Training, Students from the Law of Attraction Training Center, 'Truth vs. Falsehood' by Dr David Hawkins MD, 'The Amazing Power of Deliberate Intent' by Esther, Jerry & Abraham Hicks.

Each section is often in a different colour.

After questioning your position on the scale, consider that you have a choice. A positive outcome for you if you can allow forgiveness to be part of a healing process. There is no magic wand, no magic time scale, only a probable realisation and understanding that it would be good to feel the warmth and beauty of what is around you. Surely, that has to be a lovely thought!

Grief

Grief is a multi-faceted response to loss, particularly to the loss of someone or something to which a bond was formed.

Examples of feelings and beliefs around grief:

- I am useless and not want to be alone.
- I will not be strong enough to deal with the responsibilities of life on my own.
- Gosh, I got let off the hook. Can I deal with that?

There are countless beliefs around death.

I remember a Cruse Counsellor telling me that it was recommended to wait several months after my trauma before I should consider or would be considered for counselling. That was fine with me. Perhaps not fine for others who wish to have the offer of support when the pain is at its most acute. I think that time does need to pass for counselling to be of real value. The peak distress, pain and anguish need to be reduced. This is purely my opinion.

There is no right or wrong way to grieve. It is obviously individual. Sudden death is very shocking and unexpected. Anticipated grief in relation to someone's long-term illness, is horribly difficult too. There are many aspects – anger, unfairness, rage, sadness, fear.

Spiritual understanding and permitting a move beyond the physical pain when struck by grief takes time. There denial.

For further reading David Kessler and Elizabeth Kubler-

Ross write about the five stages of grief:

grief.com/the-five-stages-of-grief

Denial, anger, bargaining, depression, and acceptance – a process which has no set order. One piece of great advice shared by many is that we should cry. It is a wonderful release. To cry until we are unable to cry any longer.

I found it almost impossible to cry. I maintain I was stunned and shocked by the final outcome. (A freeze response.) I dare say that I could still work on that feeling but I have moved on. An old film will make me cry and sometimes other people's misfortunes have the same effect.

I still have a protective shield around me. It keeps me safe but I have shed many layers!

You too can shed layers. If you have done so, that's wonderful. Be proud that you have moved on. A whole world of opportunity can come your way. You are not blocking it.

Working with EFT and Matrix does not take away the natural grieving process, but it certainly can help when you are ready to move forward in your life: when you seek help to achieve a freedom from 'the ties which bind'.

Question: Is it time to move on after grief?

Clean questions: What would you like to have happen? What needs to happen for that to happen?

Death and Dying

The fear of death.

When I was about to tackle this subject, I was sitting in the garden with Herb. It was a beautiful morning and we were able to eat breakfast outdoors. An ideal place to put forward this thought! I said, 'You know, I seriously believe that we are here, on earth, for a purpose. We have an allocated time. I believe and accept that but dying scares the shit out of me! I don't want to die!'

He told me to write it in the book. He told me to highlight the dilemma. Where is the logic in accepting we are here for a purpose but still remain fearful of dying? I can't offer a resource to prepare for dying so I will just share a few thoughts.

I still want plenty of time because there is so much to do and enjoy! But we all die. If we can learn from what life has dealt us and perhaps share it, then what a magical opportunity that can be.

If we are with someone whilst they are dying, we can give them peace and love and tell them how much they have meant to us. Tell them how important they were. Tom Sweetman, one of my contributors now works in this area. See www.tomletgo.com

I was with my mother, at the beginning of 2012 when she died. I managed to be with her during her last two hours. Not easy when you are told you need to get on a flight NOW!

My sister and I sat with our mother as she struggled for every breath she could take. She couldn't swallow or close her eyes. Horrible, but I swear she knew that I was there. The staff in the retirement home suggested that she was hanging on because they had told her I was coming up to see her. It was an *honour* to be with my mother when she took her last gasp. It was a profound experience. It is said that the dying choose their time to go. Perhaps you nip to the bathroom and they take the opportunity then when they are alone.

I believe my mother thought I'd gone out of the room. I had. I shouted downstairs, (yes, in the care home at one o'clock in the morning!) to my sister, but I was keeping an eye on my mother and caught her red-handed trying to sneak off to the next world. So she had to put up with us being there. I hope she didn't mind.

One of my clients had a concern around death. From a Matrix/EFT point of view, a memory will hold the key. Find the message learned around death and work on a positive learning instead of holding the fear and dread which possibly many of us experience.

Personal Transformation

To transform: to change in form, appearance, or structure

I'm going to mention a little about personal transformation. The hype around transformation is huge. People making statements about how this, that and the other will help you transform: to be the person you may like to be.

Personal transformation is best achieved when someone's hand is up: when they are volunteering or ready to embrace change. They are already half way there. They wish something to change and have a desire to alter a way of behaviour.

It takes work, effort and a shift in the belief system to achieve personal transformation.

If unable to recognise that real work needs done, it will only be a struggle. The timing won't be right. The person will procrastinate and it's truly not worth their while.

For example: stopping smoking. I've been there and done that! Tried it a couple of times before. What a carry on! My husband tried twice and found it extremely distressing. I am now a successful non-smoker. However for me to achieve that big change, questions needed to be asked.

- Do I want to die too?
- Have I not smoked enough?

Eighteen months after he died I had my third and final attempt to stop smoking. It wasn't that difficult because I wanted to stop. I made no attempt until I was finally ready.

I suggest you try to understand why you want to change? If

you understand *why,* then you have a fighting chance of success.

Baby steps are a good way to begin:

Sometimes you need to leave or drop people from your life.

Sometimes only a simple tweak around a relationship with a friend or family member who drains you can be enough!

Find people who will support, believe and want to be with you on your journey.

I have a wonderful plaque bought in Edinburgh. It is hanging on my kitchen wall. I only show it to clients who I hope will see the 'gallows humour'.

'If you are depressed or have low self-esteem, just check that you are not surrounded by arseholes!'

Question: Are you willing to give effort to make a big change in your life?

Clean question: What do you want to have happen? What needs to happen for that to happen?

Anger

What is anger? It is suggested that real anger is an addiction. People need a 'fix' of anger in the same way that others need a fix of alcohol, drugs or caffeine.

A more general explanation of anger is that it is a 'mask' for fear, emotional pain or emotional hurt. Ponder over that should you consider you have an anger trigger.

I used to have feelings of anger and can relate to the mask explanation.

I rarely become angry. It is so debilitating. As quickly as possible I quieten myself. If necessary I will 'tap'. I detest the feeling of not caring what happens next and being potentially out of control. No one will benefit. Least of all me. I cannot function properly when angry. Who can? There is no excuse for any behaviour resulting from a fit of anger.

I could labour this but to me the explanation given covers all bases.

Questions :

What makes you angry?

Does it really make you angry or is it fear, hurt or pain that you feel?

If you are angry, do you need fixes of anger to keep you going?

*Clean question*s: Does your anger have a shape or form? Is there anything else about that anger?

Procrastination

Putting off or delaying an action to a later time.

Well! How many of us put off doing or completing things because … because we have a million and one excuses not to do it. The time wasn't right!

Of course, there are valid reasons to delay actions and those may show us better solutions, better answers, more enjoyment and success.

But … procrastination – I've procrastinated about a couple of aspects of this book. The 'who I might upset' aspect. I was fearful but I am not 'sweeping anything under the carpet' and I am trusting my judgement.

It took me a long time to decide what surname to use as author of this book. Procrastination and self-sabotage played its part. It could have allowed me to delay finishing. However, I did not permit such intervention.

Why do we put off doing something such as living our dream? Life can pass us by.

Fear can stop us. My advice is to clear that fear. I have a YouTube video 'Tapping on Fear and Panic.

www.youtube.com/watch?v=Z505GSpX99U

Question: What do you procrastinate over? What excuses do you make?

Clean question: What do you want to have happen? What needs to happen for that to happen?

Dealing with Alcoholism

'a mental obsession that causes a physical compulsion to drink.'

Alcoholism has been recognized for many years by professional medical organizations as a primary, chronic, progressive and sometimes fatal disease.

I would not be comfortable working with an alcoholic. I will work with those abused by or supporting an alcoholic. However I suggest that eventually they may see they are wasting their time, punishing themselves because the alcoholic may have to be crawling in the gutter before finally attempting to get up and take action. Alcoholics generally blame anyone but themselves. An alcohol addiction has deep roots. An addictive person does not like him or herself. It is so easy to kill the pain by just having that next small drink: to feed the inadequacy.

To succeed in overcoming addiction the addictive person faces considerable challenge.

What makes someone an alcoholic or some form of addict? My thoughts and my experience with my husband are my only knowledge.

Perhaps consider this analogy:

The small child who is given a sweetie to placate, to feel good. As the child grows, a bigger sweetie is required. The sweetie makes them feel better, happier, loved, safe, secure. The prize, the reward required to feel good, grows.

My message: The emotional scars from living with an alcoholic do not need to dictate how you live the rest of your life.

You do not have the answers. Should you believe that it is your fault, your responsibility, you too are playing a 'victim' role. And that's not a pretty role.

Question: Is there an alcoholic involved somewhere in your life? Are you able to deal with it? If not …

Clean questions: What do you want to have happen? What needs to happen for that to happen? Is there anything else about that?

Physical pain

Whilst training in EFT and Matrix Reimprinting, one statement surprised me.

It is considered that physical pain and disease is up to 90 per cent related to emotional pain (stress) held in the body.

EFT and Matrix Reimprinting Energy Healing can be hugely beneficial in clearing negative emotions held in the body as a result of trauma.

Here are some resources to consider:

- Dr Bruce Lipton is an internationally recognised leader in bridging science and spirit. His talks combine cutting-edge science, mind body medicine and spiritual principles. There are many YouTube clips on this.

- Louise Hay, author of 'You Can Heal Your Life', and Bruce Lipton tell us that physical symptoms are tangible evidence of what is going on in our unconscious mind, showing us how we really feel, deep inside. If this book title is new to you then I suggest you go out and buy it today.

- I find Meta Medicine very interesting. A book linked to Meta Medicine is *'The Biogenealogy Sourcebook - Healing the Body by Resolving Traumas of the Past'.*by Christian Fleche.

Question: If you can accept that emotional pain is hugely responsible for physical pain and disease, can you recognise that potentially this could be happening to you or to someone you know?

*Clean question*s So if emotional distress affects physical health what needs to happen? Then what happens?

Other resources

Meditation and relaxation techniques

'Enlightenment is an accident
Meditation makes you more accident prone.'

If I have difficulty sleeping a meditation or relaxation audio will help me 'nod off'. These audios serve two purposes. They help me sleep and the message enters my subconscious as it is repeated, gaining strength.

Mindset

Dr Michelle Hanisch. When I googled *Mindset* I discovered Michelle. I instantly loved the way she wrote about the difficult emotional stuff which can weigh us down. I read her blogs and suggest that you have a read. She is Australian and I like her no-nonsense but warm style of writing.

www.healgrowtransform.com.au

Energy Medicine Exercises

Energy Medicine brings you vitality when you are drained, health when you are ill, and joy when you are down.'
Donna Eden.

I have learned basic Energy Medicine Exercises from my friend and fellow Matrixer, Paula Bishop. Paula trains in Donna Eden's Energy Medicine.

I love doing those exercises in the classroom with primary children too. Children are very open to this kind of fun activity.

Children respond extremely well to EFT. They do not have the same hang-ups as adults.

Picture Tapping Technique (PTT)

PTT is very effective with a child or an adult who has difficulty verbalising a trauma. Through metaphor and imagination problems can be released in a painless and indirect way.

Singing Bowls

Herb and I bought a Himalayan singing bowl in a French market. Sound therapy is relaxing and it centres mind and body.

Time to let go

'Let it happen. Just let it happen.'

Ted Wilmont's closing words to our Matrix training group.

You know something? When I do *just let it happen* – it does!

The Law of Attraction and Intention

If we act, behave, live our life in a positive fashion, expect good things, are open to opportunity, then generally good things do happen. We receive more harmony and success.

So when you sense a glimmer, a sign that tells you to start making moves to improve your life, please appreciate that it may now be 'time to let go.'

www.therealconfidenceguide.com

Section 3
Contributions from others now thriving
their positive messages

I consider those who have contributed their stories to be brave and confident. They are aware that they have suffered a trauma in their life. They have tackled it and have come out the other end. They believe that they can volunteer a positive message; something of value to readers. They wish you success and a brighter future. I am also acutely aware that others declined to contribute. I understand.

If someone had suggested a year ago that I would be doing this project, interviewing people, be driven to complete it, I would have chuckled and said, 'Not a chance!'

The moment I became excited and eager to start, everything fell into place. Enjoy these brave and generous contributions.

The death of my father

The story, or trauma, I would like to share is the death of my father five years ago. He died unexpectedly, of a heart attack, aged 68. He collapsed at work and died four days later, having never regained consciousness.

It was the first time anyone so close to me had died. What surprised me and what I particularly want to share is that this trauma was a very 'active' experience in that it wasn't just shock or grief that you eventually recover from, but that there were so many different facets to it, and it surprised me that some of them were so positive!

Denial did play a huge part during the initial twenty-four hours. Shock and denial. The seriousness of the situation seemed on a different level from one I could comprehend.

A first positive incident…

A few days after my Dad died, my aunt and uncle came to stay with us. Our uncle was asked to cook a meal because we knew he would prefer to be away from all the emotional stuff. The meal, for about ten of us was a good distracting challenge for him. It gave us great amusement especially as he sipped at his wine regularly. We were well entertained. He was a meticulous cook, whereas my father was a 'pans everywhere' cook. And it struck me that we would never have had that entertainment if my Dad had been around because he would have been the one doing the cooking.

An important realisation…

I realised my Dad had to die before I could see that all my life I had been jealous of the attention he gave to my brother. Of course, once my Dad wasn't around, there was nothing to be jealous of any more. And although we have never discussed it, I know something shifted for my brother too because one evening a few days after the heart attack, I remember looking across the table at him and he had a look on his face that I can only describe as love.

I had no formal help to manage my grief but I did have lots of support from my siblings, their partners, other family and my friends. I couldn't have done it without them. That time felt like I was living in a bubble: a slightly surreal experience.

We are five years down the line now and we are all okay, including my Mum. She needs a lot of emotional support which she gets and as for her drinking, well she still overindulges now and again but she has taken control herself because she does not have Dad to rely on now. She has become quite independent and she travels by bus and airplane to visit me. My Dad would be really proud of her.

Allison Galbraith – Macintosh Wright

Birth of a child without a future
– death of hope, dreams

My son was born with Cystic Fibrosis: Life limiting and degenerative. It can only get worse. There is no cure and life expectancy is unknown – five years, ten years or thirty years. When he was born, I lost my horizon. We assume we raise a child to eighteen. I did not have that horizon.

So very many conflicting emotions and thoughts disturbed me when he was a baby:

As he matures he would always be dependent on me financially and emotionally to see him through to the end of his illness.

I was never going to be independent of my child and at that time, I felt it was a prison sentence. No remission.

There was the total love a mother has for her new baby and the total dread and fear of dealing with this alone because I knew my husband was going to be totally useless.

I was in a downward spiral, thinking that this was the end of my life and it was all for nothing.

However, my thoughts were also: 'I will deal with it. I know I'm strong enough to deal with it.'

The only advice I was given was to live each day at a time. Impossible for someone who has to run a busy house, a full time career and has had to plan everything. Suddenly, you can't plan at all. Everybody is affected by it. I can only describe it as standing in quick sand.

Everyone else went back to work, or to their routine. I felt isolated, lonely. The doctor told me the only thing which would affect my son's outcome was how well I could care for him: the physiotherapy, drugs, care and attention were all now down to me.

Q. How did that affect you?

Ten years later, I was treated for acute depression.

I found myself looking at life from a parallel track. The view from my track was the same as everyone else's but I can never go back to the other side. I will always now, on a daily basis, have to deal with the prospect of the death of my child. I may have looked happy and believed I was happy, but I could never be truly happy again. I became quite hardened and disengaged. I was difficult to be around. I was constantly working harder to keep in control and subsequently became depressed.

Many weeks at a time would be spent in hospital. It was hard for everyone and although I did not want to have this problem, I did not want to be without my child. So I was treated for depression with drugs and counselling but not nearly enough counselling. The financial costs were high for me. My budget was stretched. I was paying for my two daughters to go to boarding school because I had to spend so much time in hospital with my son, sleeping there, sitting there. I had a mortgage to pay and my husband was 'just not able to work' with the stress his life was under. Somehow, I managed to manoeuvre all that my high-powered job required. I had to keep my job.

I got into debt and had to take out a second mortgage. I finished off isolated, anxious and had this mountain to climb and I had to climb it every day. The marriage suffered. It was clear there was no room for someone who was not pulling their weight.

For the first five years after my divorce I was happier. I wasn't propping up a man who also suffered from depression. When my son was growing into adolescence, and learning to cope with his illness himself, I then worked on paying off my debt, rebuilding and trying to participate in a normal life again. It's hard finding the right people who can support you.

Q. Where has it left you?

I am now on the other side of an abyss. I never look back. The depression is like a black dog that you know is behind you but I don't ever want those feelings again of 'the blackness, the I can't believe I've woken up again, that I'm still alive, that I'd do anything just to die, but without killing myself'.

Q. How do you get through a day?

I had to put safe boundaries around myself. I couldn't overdo it. I admitted when I was tired when I couldn't do it, when it was too much for me. I asked for help. I shared with people how bleak it was.

I had to lose the people from my 'first life' because they couldn't handle it; they did not want to hear. I had to find people who were willing, open and able to ask me to share it with them : A whole different kind of people. I was given two visualisations by a psychologist so that I could confront this life of mine at my own pace.

Metaphorically, I put all the troubles, difficulties, fears into a box, a box in a cupboard.

I could *look* into it sometimes, slowly, at my own pace.

I could also have a *good look* at all the stuff in the box to see how well I was dealing with everything related to Cystic Fibrosis.

Or ... the Cystic Fibrosis (CF) could be like a coat. I could confront it very slowly at my own pace. I could choose *when* to put the coat on. When I took it off, I could visualise being someone else.

If there was a two-week hospital spell when my son was ill, I put on the C.F coat and walked with that, for that time. In the earlier days, the coat would have been on all the time. The dread and fear. I don't need to work with 'the coat' visualisation any more.

In my mind, I was always planning to bury my child. In fact, that may not be the case. I have had to change my mind set. Be brave enough to hope. I have had a couple of years respite and I may have another ten years. My life revolves around his hospital visits and stays: On-going and chronic. It comes and goes.

A Positive Message

If you can find one or two stepping stones, that's all it takes to get your foot on the first stepping stone – out of the bleakness and a reason to find that stone and start walking.

When you reach crisis point, the resources are there.

Things can turn around.
My GP was fantastic.
The NHS was fantastic.

I had a personal trainer. I used to run myself into the ground to deal with the pain of it all. She made me write lists after my run about all the things I had to get done. She recognised I needed support. She gave me tasks I had to do. She did not need to do this. It was not her role, but she helped me.

I found an excellent organisation, Community Service Volunteers (CSV)[5] through the local authority. They provided a carer. This was amazing and made such a difference.

I have two beautiful daughters. I am married again to someone who is big enough to understand and able not to compete with the complexities and demands of what I have to do with my son.

Time helps too, of course. My son had grown with this. He is a man. He no longer needs me in that emotional context any more. He asks for my help when he needs it.

I have given away my ambition and certain material possessions. I accepted that my life is defined by other factors other than what I could have done. I let it go. I have other priorities and I am now much more relaxed about my future. The job I have now does not stress me out. It fits around my life. If I have to rearrange my timetable, I can. I don't need to reschedule board meetings, tell untruths. I run my own business. My view of my world and what constitutes a good life is different.

---

[5] Charity dedicated to giving everyone the chance to play an active part in their community through volunteering, training, education and the media.

I was warned by my doctor that I would emerge from counselling a different person and I should be prepared for that. In the past I had taken on jobs, really big, powerful jobs and was big and bold enough to do it, without thinking about the stress and how it would affect me. After the meltdown and being off work for six months with depression, I de-stressed my life completely.

But of course, I then needed challenges. The difference is I know when I am feeling my stress levels rise and I stop going any further with whatever it is. I find that quite liberating and have no qualms about saying, 'No, that's my boundary reached. If I go any further I could get pulled into the abyss again.' I am not going to do that.

Anon

The positive drive
to overcome a serious car accident

Dean is very positive about his message and inspires many people, especially those who know him as a Personal Instructor.

In 2001, aged seventeen, Dean was a passenger in a car involved in a very serious traffic accident : hitting a double-decker bus head on. No drink or drugs were involved just sadly the inexperience of a young driver with a fairly powerful car. His friend, the driver, was killed and Dean was hospitalised for many weeks.

He was kept in an induced coma for three weeks and then had some time in recovery.

His injuries were:

Frontal lobe brain damage: it controls emotions and personality.

Serious hand damage.

Double fracture of skull, eye out of socket, collarbone broken, lung collapsed.

He was paralysed from the neck down and was in an induced coma to allow the brain to repair and heal.

After being brought round, his family were warned of potential brain damage.

He is aware he is very fortunate to be alive.

Q. What is his attitude to life now?

Before the accident, he was training to be a graphic designer. Dean's memory was that the brain surgeon told him not to expect too much. This just made him decide to prove the doctors and anyone else who shared that message, wrong. He was not interested in being told what he could and couldn't hope to achieve. Any negative suggestions were turned into positive efforts.

He suffered weight and muscle loss. He was in a wheelchair because he couldn't walk. The medical people needed to do tests. Dean asked for them to be done straight away. He felt the medical people were very negative. Again his attitude was to prove them wrong.

Possible alterations to staircases and moving his bedroom downstairs were mentioned to his parents. Dean's attitude was 'No. If I can't walk up stairs, I'll crawl up.'

They were trying to class him as disabled and this constantly made him strive to prove them wrong.

Q. Do you have any disability now?

No.

The recovery process was slow and everything was achieved in baby steps. In the first two years, his short-term memory was problematic. He could not recognise newer friends but did recognise close family. He was given puzzles and tasks which little children are given. He felt that his brain was like a big jigsaw puzzle where many pieces of the puzzle were missing. But when one piece fitted in, it brought back other pieces with it. He had been dyslexic and this had worsened. He saw a psychiatrist and a speech therapist for about five years. It was all done in baby steps – daunting but successful.

Q. Where is he now? Is he living a normal life?

Yes, Dean shares his own home with his fiancée, and their baby son.

Q. So what worked for him?

Dean states that the thing that really got him to where he is today is fitness, exercise.

Around eight months after the accident, Dean went back to his graphic design course – a few hours at a time, mainly to try to get back to some form of normality and social interaction. He finished the course and his results were good but he hoped for better. Dean admitted to being a bit of a perfectionist and has always tried to be the best he can be!

He also knew that he really wanted to be a Personal Trainer because he did a lot of his own rehabilitation. The NHS rehab was great for the elderly but he felt he wasn't pushed hard enough. He motivated himself. He wanted to feel a 'good sweat'!

To regain his strength he started with swimming. He had been a lifeguard at a local pool. His job had been kept open and he was allowed to use the facilities free of charge. He swam regularly, three times a week, for up to a year. The next step forward took him to the gym. A GP referral allowed him to visit three times a week. After that, he would attend the gym five days a week. He had to cycle half an hour there and back. He then worked there as a gym instructor for two years. He now works at Fitness First as a Personal Instructor.

He got his driving licence back when proved fit. He drives and rides a motorbike now too. The accident holds no fear regarding driving and motorbike riding. Life is for living!

Dean is rightly very pleased with his recovery and where he is in his life today. He promotes positivity. He believes his story and his success undoubtedly helps to motivate his clients. He is happy to have included the more graphic detail. He believes the reader can become more involved, possibly relate to it and learn.

He wants to show people they can succeed if they are prepared to put their mind to the task.

Dean Whitfield, Personal Trainer at Fitness First, Bognor Regis. Deansfitness@gmail.com

A terrifying knife attack in her home

This lady lived in South Africa for many years and was the target of a premeditated robbery. She believes that her long-term maid was in cahoots or had been bullied into tricking her, to allow 'a friend' to enter her secure home.

During the brutal attack and robbery, she believed she would be killed. Threats were made to her life. She feared rape. She feared Aids.

Police and the psychiatrist remarked on her strength of character after the event. She did respect the fact that her body was in shock and needed time to heal. She was prescribed medication but chose to stop taking it after a few days.

However, her home, her 'place of beauty' was now a place of fear. She put the house on the market at the end of that week and she and her husband had moved home within a month. In South Africa, moving house is straightforward.

A year later whilst out driving, she recognised the man who had attacked her. She *calmly* ignored him and reported the fact to the police. He was arrested and eventually the case was dealt with. The trauma of attending the court was awful for her. She was mixing with the likes of child rapists. These child rapists hold the belief that if they have sex with a child this will cure them of Aids. This was a very traumatic episode but she undertook no medication or treatment.

As a result:

She left South Africa to come to Britain to feel safer. This has been a very *positive* move.

She does not waste her time being unforgiving. She has moved on.

Fear was the issue. She is careful and aware of this potential pitfall and does not dwell on the past.

She emphasises that she is most definitely a survivor, not a casualty.

She states that shock has a physical effect on the body and we should be respectful of that.

She is cross when people might suggest she must have been attracting the negative into her life.

Living in South Africa is hazardous in many respects. She was happy. She was successful. She had a lovely house and was starting a new business. The event came 'out of the blue'.

As soon as she had moved to her new apartment in South Africa her life turned around and many good things happened. She was in a good place. New doors opened. Successful business opportunities came her way. The fact that she came to Britain to deal with her fear is just part of her journey.

Her message: 'I am in a good place. Do not dwell on the past. Be strong.'

Anon

Adopted

When Isobel was nine years old her adoptive father died. He had been ill for a year and the seriousness of the illness had been kept from her. To protect her. She was sent to school the next day as normal; as if nothing out of the ordinary had happened. The message she learned: carry on as normal – stiff upper lip attitude.

When she was seventeen her adoptive mother died. She missed her undoubtedly, but got on with her life.

She was married for seventeen years and prone to some spells of postnatal depression.

At thirty-four, she entered into another relationship, an aggressive relationship. At this time, she also felt bullied at work. She sought counselling, talk therapy, and highly praised the counselling she was given.

Although Isobel was attending sessions with regard to relationship issues, on her first visit it was suggested that she had not dealt with the death of her adoptive parents. She was completely and utterly surprised by her reaction: she just howled. She said she was surprised by the noise she heard herself making; she sounded like a wounded animal. She could not believe she was harbouring all this pent-up emotion.

On her second visit, she howled and cried again, releasing years of pent-up emotions. She realised that she had missed her parents enormously.

On the third visit, she saw a different man and was delighted to work with him too. It was suggested she was clinging on to the aggressive relationship because she was frightened of losing people. She had not been *allowed* to grieve when her parents had died and so had never really healed. She may have been holding on to this abusive relationship as a source of having someone to love her.

Her message: 'Love yourself. That is vital. Don't rely on others to love you; start by liking and loving yourself. If you can't or don't love yourself, everything else will just eat away at you.'

You may have to work at this. Try to speak to others. Counselling is really a very good way to 'offload'.

Isobel did not want someone to be judgemental with her. She wanted people to listen. When they did and she was allowed *to speak,* her confidence grew.

Interview published with Isobel's approval

Redundancy and Industrial Tribunal

Following a very stressful two years, including a one year build up to the inevitable redundancy I was eventually made redundant from my job in June 2011. With all that and the prospect of a tribunal I was extremely distressed and very depressed. I couldn't sleep or eat and used the Healing Codes[6] daily.

Doing a healing code before tribunal meetings allowed me to remain calm and to retain my power and control.

Having trained in EFT myself I know the benefits that tapping can bring. However, I needed the support of another practitioner to help me work through the emotions I was feeling. I had five EFT / Matrix Reimprinting sessions with Susan. The Matrix Reimprinting helped rebuild my self-esteem and confidence. I discovered that some emotional debris from early childhood memories had reinforced some negative issues around the tribunal.

I am continuing on my healing journey and, as yet, have not looked for work or set up my own EFT / Reconnective Healing practice. I see this healing time as the equivalent of Eckhart Tolle's [7] two years out on a park bench, people watching and learning to be in the moment.

EFT, Matrix Reimprinting and the Healing Codes complement Mindfulness practice and support meditation.

Maria Kielty

---

[6] The Healing Codes are a simple and powerful self-healing system discovered in 2001 by Alex Loyd.

[7] Eckhart Tolle author of '*The Power of Now*'

The beauty in death

*'Tom, I have no regrets and did everything I wanted;
make sure you live your life to the fullest.'*
were mum's last words to me

Life for me has been a journey of many roads. Sometimes I have driven well and the journey was good. Other times I have misjudged the bend, gone off the road, been stranded with no breakdown recovery insurance.

A life changing event put me back on course. In April of 2012 after four years of dealing with her cancer, my mum passed away. It shocked me to the core. Months had been spent at the hospice experiencing grief which had left me feeling lonely, afraid, numb, and with a sense of thinking that I was not going to be able to carry on. I had truly come to one of life's blocked roads. Trapped and stranded with no one seeing or hearing me. It was in this moment after her death, I realised I had to let go of everything I was thinking – things that were holding me back. I must allow for change to find a way through.

At the funeral, the church was full. I realised how much one person can affect a whole community. Many people were sharing my mum's legacy and I saw how she had made an impact on their lives in some way. It also started to show me a hidden beauty and in the following months, I had a shift, a major turning point leading to great realisation.

I needed to have a greater understanding of grief: a process which I would then share when assisting others suffering from the death of a loved one. I wished to be able to shed new light on how they feel and use it to empower them to move on. I wished them to be able to honour the life of their loved one and to be able to feel gratitude and love instead of grief and loss.

The death of my mum has led to the birth of my life's work. I have purpose and to me it is a gift for which I am deeply grateful. It has provided me with a path to follow and such a clear road map. I believe I know what is on, and also what is in, the way.

The work I now do is providing grief transformations through my 'Let Go Process'. It assists others in transforming their experience of death and loss. I would like to share with you two thoughts which may empower you on your journey when coping with grief.

'When listening to others, try to sit and be a witness to them in a place of non-judgement. Remember we are human 'being' and a lot of the time, we forget this and become human thinking and human doing. Deeper connections arise when we are present with someone.'

'One of the biggest insights I had when my mum was in the hospice was that during the times we find difficult and painful, we can later become empowered. We can raise our self-awareness, and trust that we can let go of the grief and pain.'

Tom Sweetman

Please visit me at:
www.tomletgo.com and
www.facebook.com/tomletgo

How life can change dramatically.
Insights: A car accident and loss of a limb.

In 2001, I had a 'successful life': nice house, car, wife and children and a successful business, and then bang, my life was turned upside down. I had a serious car accident resulting in the amputation of my arm. My business partner terminated my directorship whilst I was in hospital and MRSA (the superbug bacteria) and other complications meant that my physical recovery took two years. A costly litigation exercise fortunately enabled me to get a fair recompense for my shareholding.

These are my lessons learned from the different experiences along the way.

The 7 steps to the meaning of life:

1. When the shit hits the fan, your priorities change: In normal life there can be seemingly hundreds of different things to worry about, yet as soon as I had a major car accident and was fighting for my very survival, all of the hundreds of little problems disappeared in an instant to be replaced with laser sharp focus on a minimal number of priorities. It's a matter of perspective. When you know what's really important for you and you make those the priorities and nothing else, the resultant clarity and effectiveness can produce some stunning results.

2. When you spend a lot of time in hospital you gain humility: I used to be self- assured and very arrogant. After weeks in hospital struggling for my life I realised we are all the same and all have our own crosses to bear from the lofty consultants to the next person to leave the ward in a body bag. At base level despite all the different societal labels, we are human beings

trying to do the best we can with what we've got. Once you understand this at a knowing level, it's difficult to be so arrogant again.

3.   Sometimes you need to move away from bad energy sources: However despite being all flesh and blood we tread different paths, and when someone's negativity is so great, it's best to simply move away. I had a particular experience in an amputee clinic waiting room when a particular woman (double leg amputee, very obese and stuffing herself with food) could do nothing but complain with bad attitude about anything she could find to complain about. I found it necessary to physically move as far away as possible so as not be contaminated and influenced by her behaviour. The old adage about being careful of the company you keep is certainly true.

4.   Sometimes a simple compass point goal and baby steps is better than SMART goals: One day when returning from weeks in hospital I was so weak that it took me five minutes to climb a single flight of stairs. This was a wake-up call. I quickly decided to get fit. That was it, nothing specific, measurable or time bound, just a simple compass point to aim for, something that gave me some direction and purpose in a time of great weakness. What I then did was take baby steps in that given direction as and when I felt I could without any laid out plan. This started with getting to the letterbox at the end of the road and back. Gradually I moved further and faster in a non-linear way until two years later, I completed an Olympic distance triathlon. I achieved far more than I could have possibly thought realistically achievable at the outset. Such is the power of simple goals and baby steps.

5. One man bands don't work: None of us have a full skill set. And to run any business requires the full set. What's more, for most people it's easier to be accountable to someone else than to ourselves. For this reason, I believe it's essential to design and create partnerships and teams, virtual or otherwise, to support you in your business venture.

6. Make conscious trade-offs: Perhaps this is the summation of all the experiences above. Trying to 'have it all' is guaranteed to disappoint because to get the benefits of focus and prioritisation, the tenacity to keep the baby steps going in the same direction, the compromises created when working as part of a team, you have to make trade-offs. When you're young you make them easily because you're often blissfully unaware of the negative consequences and also don't have as many options available to you, but even as it gets harder as you get older, conscious trade-offs are needed all the same. The allure of 'having it all' is all the stronger but don't let it fool you.

7. It appears that life can give you setbacks which allow the opportunity to make better conscious choices: But in my experience don't expect these choices to become clear in an instant. If it were that easy we'd all have life sorted! Revisiting steps 1 to 6 will help, as these steps are easily forgotten when life is going well!

Tim Johnson

www.Tim-Johnson.co.uk

A divorce

When we meet as parents, we can discuss the children in a civil manner and most of the time we both want the same thing for them. There is agreement about that at least. Those short meetings can make me feel good but at no time have I wished to be back in the relationship. I know it is much better now, being apart.

Health point of view.

I have put on weight so that may show that I am happier. I was underweight before and assumed that was just me. But I then realised that I was probably living on adrenalin and nervous tension. I don't eat any more food now than before, but people are very positive about how I look with regard to the gain in weight.

I have always believed I am a strong person but sometimes I don't know how I managed to find my way through the distressing times. Others have crumbled and fallen in similar situations.

Q. What might have helped you get through it?

Work was the answer. I throw myself into work and do what I need to do. I maintain and keep a good relationship with my clients. I may do a bit of burying my head in the sand. Nowadays I don't have to go into the office regularly and put on a brave face, I just seem to have sorted my way through it all.

Although things are improving, we share responsibility of the children. The children share their lives between us. This seems to work as well as can be expected. However, it does not make me happy. I would like to have my children with me every day. On the mornings when I wake up and they are not with me, it saddens me. That's my loss in this horrible situation.

But my life is somewhat easier because I do have some respite. My older child is a teenager and finds the set-up quite stressful. The younger child is still quite young and adapts better to the situation. So from that point of view, sharing is easier. It is a situation where we have been able to accommodate the needs or wishes of our children. I am becoming more used to our set-up. I have a routine.

I have discussions with my older child, stating that I love them both totally.   I share my hopes for them and I hope to reassure. I try to reach out – to reinforce those facts. We both love our children. However, sharing my children is not being a complete mother in my opinion. But it is my situation.

Re: Men and other relationships

It would be nice to go out with someone to the cinema, for a drink, a meal but without all the other stuff such as:

the starting again

telling the life story

discussing the baggage.

So I am not looking for a relationship. I am happy on my own. Sharing time with someone would be nice but it's not a deep need.

One thing I would like to be different is having an improved babysitting solution. I don't have that at the moment and can feel restricted. My circle of friends is not greatly helpful in that respect. I would also like a social group of friends, something that does not require my needing a man. So it is learning, accepting and a hopefully improving situation.

Our marriage did not have domestic violence or anything ghastly like that. It simply wasn't working. We could both have benefited from sorting this all out at least two years before we did. The financial situation caused us concern. Who leaves? Who goes first? Finally, it was the financial problems that allowed me to get out of the marriage.

Q. What are you doing now?

I enjoy Zumba because I realised that poor eating and drinking is not helpful in the long run. So I make time for Zumba and it helps me to feel better.

In the past I may have considered what my husband might say when I tried different things. I felt I had someone to please, to placate, to consider. And I don't have that now. I can do something because I want to do something.

I've done things to my hair! Bought and wear new clothes and keep fit. It all boils down to feeling more confident. Baby steps. Finding *me* again. Confident and increasing my confidence.

Anon

Boyfriend's attempted suicide

This female contributor lived with her partner. She was wakened in the night to find her boyfriend's father in the house. He had been called by his son because his son was attempting suicide. She found them in the bathroom. The cry for help was really aimed at his father. The father was the financial provider for his business but he also craved his father's emotional support. She was the one having to deal with it all.

Contributing circumstances: her partner being made redundant; becoming somewhat depressed; having other jobs which did not last; drinking quite heavily.

At that point, this woman realised that she was unhappy with all that was going on, and there were additional knock-on factors: a serious accident, suffered considerable pain, dependency on painkillers, anti-depressants, pressure of business. And a childlike need for emotional support from his father which was not given.

With all of the above going on, she questioned what she was doing in this relationship. She was aware or believed that his drug-taking and depression was half illness and half personality.

And heavy drinking was still going on. She was aware that

if he really wanted to help himself he would. On an emotional level, his father was a wholly negative figure.

The attempted suicide was a scream for his dad's support. He was unhappy with his father's life. The father had found a new woman and the son felt 'lost'.

As a result of these contributing factors, her partner was

placed in a psychiatric unit of a well-known establishment for abuse dependency.

This was an unpleasant situation and visiting was deeply distressing. She was also attempting to keep his business running. She had to lie to all his business associates and staff as she tried to keep the business afloat. She was dragged down and very stressed. Trying to remember all the variation of lies was hugely unpleasant. The father was not supportive and the boyfriend was happy to stay in rehab because he was getting lots of attention.

She wanted out, and to be out guilt-free. Suicide was in his family genes. Her partner's attempted suicide was not a surprise within the family – not a first. She was fearful of becoming a mother like figure and carer to him. She knew she would not take on that role. The visits to the rehab establishment were awful. Not somewhere to take a child. She believed that some patients were ill and some just wanted the attention.

Q. Her thoughts on her decision to leave the relationship.

She believed then and believes now that many people do have a choice about the life they can live. If you are in a position to make a choice, then make a good one for yourself. She did not have to stay with him. She made the choice to leave. The life that loomed ahead was not for her. Overwhelming thoughts of how to get out of it were a concern. Initially she was worried what people might think. She assumed people who did not know the whole story would be thinking:

- poor man
- an awful accident and the girlfriend can't cope

She also did not want to be responsible if he tried suicide another time, and got it right!

After the decision to leave her partner, she felt relief. She still received calls from his family members asking for her continued support. They wanted to rely on her but she was having none of it. She was out of the emotional relationship. However, it took time before she could leave the business relationship they still shared.

She was now in the position of looking forward to a new life: her own destiny and not beholding to anyone. That excited her. She never worried about being a girl on her own: Much happier to be single than miserable with someone.

One of the main reasons she was able to escape was due to the unquestioning support she received from her parents. She felt very lucky in that respect and put on her practical head to deal with conflicting emotions. When the dust finally settled, she did hit a brick wall.

She now happily married, self-employed and enjoying success.

Time is a healer.

Anon

Losing a partner to the Big C

In the late 1980s I was engaged and living with my fiancée for about four years. She battled with breast cancer for the last two years of our relationship. When she died, her two young children were then brought up by their father and grandparents.

Q. How did you deal with it?

I blocked it, right from the first diagnosis. I focused more effort in work than home life. In terms of her medical treatment and care, I avoided involvement as much as possible. We didn't talk about the future.

Soon after her death, the day before the funeral actually, I decided that I would do something for charity. I enjoy cycling, so I pledged that for one year, for each mile I rode, I would donate a pound to charity. I rode alone or with friends. On my longest journey, over the mountains from Turin to St Tropez, I was supported by my best friend. My target was 1,000 miles. I achieved over 1300 miles. It was my way of saying goodbye.

Q. What happened afterwards?

The next winter I had two skiing holidays. On the second holiday I met someone who I married a year later. Little did I know it, but my fiancée's death was no longer going to be the most horrible episode of my life.

Marrying on the rebound

I married someone I should not have married. I'd been engaged twice before. Third time lucky? No!

It was a constant challenge. My wife had told me that she

could not have children. I accepted that. Then she decided she did want children and I found out that I probably could not father a child. It was already an unsettled relationship. This additional aggravation compounded it.

Q. How did you deal with that?

We didn't! We would go down to the pub, drink too much, and then quarrel when we got home. I mostly received a verbal battering. When it got too much or she got violent, I escaped in the middle of the night, taking refuge for a few hours at the office.

I should have divorced her. I naively hoped that she would just walk away. But she waited for what seemed an eternity, then divorced me, and got half of everything. I was fairly cheesed off.

Q. What possible message of encouragement can you give as a learning from those two different and difficult relationships?

When someone has a terminal illness (such as cancer) you can't walk away from it, not if you love them. You must wait until their suffering ends, then move on.

When a relationship goes wrong and it can't be fixed then you should end it. You cannot change another person. It has to be finished.

I knew my marriage was going to end. It just didn't end fast enough. We dragged it out for a long period of time. Many do. It's such a waste.

After the divorce, I had to move home. It was a clean break. I chose to stay near my friends. I did not have to worry about seeing my ex again. It was easy because there were no children involved. It's probably much harder for those who have children. I kept the cats.

Q. Where are you now?

I don't dwell on the past, but look forward to the future. I'm in another relationship with someone who I do love dearly. We both have our faults and idiosyncrasies, but these won't stop us from sealing the relationship in 2013.

Herb

And finally

Here are two separate comments I was given by people who have declined input but who I know to be truly remarkable.

'I did things I never thought I could or would ever be called on to do. I thought I'd never be happy again. But the way I am now is like I've embraced another part of myself ... calmer, deeper, more accepting ... spiritual in a way.'

'You can't ever get over something like this, but life goes on ... I experience black days. I allow them and then I have good days.'

Author's surprise!
What I am doing now!

Perhaps, as a result of writing this book, I am getting married later this year.

When I tell people, they smile. They have a happy look on their face. When anyone has a smile, they radiate warmth and it is contagious.

I put off making the decision for quite a considerable time. I still question a need to marry. My children ask if I am doing it for the correct reason. I know that they mean: Do I love my partner? The answer is yes, I love him but we 'experienced in life' people also appreciate other reasons to marry.

However, now that I have made the decision, I am happy, relaxed and excited. I do not need to hold onto my fear any more. No more 'keeping myself safe, just in case it should go wrong'.

Readers, life is too short, open the door to opportunities. Many positive things tumble into your life when you have made space for it –.Don't take too long to choose *happier.*

Susan Cowe
soon to be Susan Miller

Bonuses

Visit www.surviveandthriveaftertrauma.com

for the following bonuses.

1. A 'Stress and Anxiety' questionnaire

Could you be suffering from an emotional overload? Here are examples of the questions. Take a few minutes and answer these questions, as honestly as you can.

- Do niggling thoughts keep you awake at night?
- Do you have trouble sleeping, but don't know why?
- Are you aware of feeling fearful, angry or sad, and don't want to?

2. A personal CD and/or Video plus a downloadable EFT tapping points resource sheet – specific to trauma.

This highlights how obstacles are simply not there when confidence and belief is felt deep within us. Freedom from emotional distress allows freedom in your life. Confidence flows and life appears easier.

3. An article on Matrix Reimprinting

By Karl Dawson, the creator of Matrix Reimprinting, an extension of EFT.

4. I will be offering my POWER mentoring

programme, for emotional well-being:

> **P**ositive
> **O**pportunities
> **W**ell-being
> **E**nergy Healing
> **R**eal Confidence

About Susan Cowe

Susan is an EFT and Matrix Reimprinting Practitioner, Reiki Practitioner and has counselling skills. She gives talks, runs workshops and has featured on TV and radio.

Susan worked as a primary teacher for over thirty years and still does a little supply teaching. Her main joy is working with clients who recognise a need for an emotional change in their lives: when something is fundamentally causing distress and there is a need to find confidence and self-belief to make the transformation.

Survive and Thrive after Trauma speaks for itself. Susan finally wrote this book once she recognised that quite simply it needed to be written.

Her partner often asked her when she was going to start the first chapter. Susan would make a hand gesture, give a shrug which indicated that the project was not immediately forthcoming. Then one day it just seemed easy.

She has a question for you: If your life could be better, what do you need to have happen?

Life is short. It can pass us by and that is a tragedy.

Susan is Scottish and lives in Hampshire, England. She has a son and a daughter who she loves without question.

She is about to marry in 2013. This is her big step.

What is yours?

Visit my websites:

www.surviveandthriveaftertrauma.com

www.therealconfidenceguide.com

www.hampshire-eft.co.uk

www.susancowereiki.co.uk

Follow me on:

Facebook - Hampshire.EFT

Twitter @SusanCowe

LinkedIn - SusanCoweEFT

YouTube - SusanCowe

Write to me at:

susan@hampshire-eft.co.uk

17571763R00078

Made in the USA
Charleston, SC
17 February 2013